DRIVE YOURSELF HAPPY

A Motor–vational Maintenance Manual

For Maneuvering Through Life

Rhonda Hull, Ph.D.

Dear Vicki and Jim ~
Savor every moment of
the journey. Choose joy
and travel with an
open heart!
♥ Rhonda Hull

Foreword by Richard Carlson
Author of *Don't Sweat the Small Stuff ... and it's all small stuff*

DRIVE YOURSELF HAPPY
A Motor–vational Maintenance Manual
For Maneuvering Through Life

Copyright ©2002 by Rhonda Hull
Printed in Canada

For information on speaking engagements
be sure to visit www.driveyourselfhappy.com

Library of Congress Cataloging–in–Publication Data

Hull, Rhonda, 1951-
    Drive yourself happy : a motor-vational maintenance manual for
maneuvering through life / by Rhonda Hull ; foreword by Richard
Carlson.– 1st ed.
    p. cm.
    ISBN 1-879384-45-0 (paper : alk. paper)
    1. Happiness. 2. Traffic signs and signals–Miscellanea. I. Title.

BF575.h27 H85 2002
158—dc21   2001052886

Hull, Rhonda.
    DRIVE YOURSELF HAPPY: A Motor–vational Maintenance
Manual for Maneuvering Through Life/ Rhonda Hull/ – 1st ed..

2   4   6   8   9   7   5   3   1

Foreword by Richard Carlson
Author of *Don't Sweat the Small Stuff...and it's all small stuff*

SADLY, IN TODAY'S WORLD, many of us either drive ourselves crazy with our own thinking, habits and frenetic behavior—or we allow others to do so. During these stressful times, it's difficult enough simply staying on track, much less dancing gracefully through life. Indeed, you almost never hear anyone saying, "I'm driving myself happy!"

That's why I was so excited to read this book and why I'm grateful for the opportunity to introduce it to you. To me, this book is a breath of fresh air. It speaks right to the heart of the matter: how to use everyday life as a "vehicle" to enrich your life. This is a fun, creative and extremely useful guide that will help all of us keep things in perspective and keep us pointed in the direction toward happiness. It's great because it takes no extra time—you simply drive, and no matter where you are on your journey, you have the insights you need to become happy!

If you're familiar with my work, you know that I believe strongly in the resiliency and inner strength of people. I'm convinced that people can learn to be happy, peaceful and caring, despite what cynics would have you believe. To me, life is a gift that becomes even more magical when you cease being irritated, bothered and frustrated. The trick is to find simple ways to either remind ourselves of something we already know and have temporarily forgotten—or to learn something new that has the capacity to heighten or change our perspective. This book offers both.

There's no question that life affords us many daily challenges and hassles. What's more, there is often a fine line between "reacting" to our challenges and "responding" to them. When we over–react, we end up overwhelmed and stressed, and we find ourselves sweating the small stuff! We get in our own way and often compound the very problems we are trying so hard to solve. On the other hand, when we respond appropriately, from a peaceful mind set, the identical set of circumstances

iii

appear quite different. Problems are solved, creativity is enhanced and productivity is increased. Obviously, it's in our best interest to become less reactive to life and more responsive to it.

But what's the secret?

The secret lies in training yourself to see things differently, to create an attitude of acceptance, gratitude, perspective, compassion and wisdom. That's what this book is all about—learning to use your daily life as an opportunity to grow and learn from your experiences rather than being overwhelmed by them.

Most of us spend at least some time each day going from one place to another. Whether in our car, on the train, bus or subway, we are presented with various road signs. To most, these signs are a necessary nuisance at best, a hassle and eye–sore at worst.

Not anymore. In *Drive Yourself Happy* you will learn to use these everyday signs in a new way. In fact, I'm fairly certain that you'll never see them the same way again. Each sign will become a reminder of an important life lesson, an insight, or a hint of perspective. The brilliance lies in the fact that you need to do little differently—you're going to be traveling anyway. It's about keeping your hands on the wheel, your eyes on the road and knowing where you're headed.

A word of caution: Don't be fooled by the clever and "cute" way Dr. Hull has packaged her material. Far from being "pollyanna–ish" or too soft, the material you are about to read has a great deal of wisdom and substance. In fact, after a single reading, I found myself happier, calmer and more able to deal effectively with my everyday life. I have no doubt that her insights will continue to inspire me.

I hope you enjoy and learn from this book as much as I have. It's a useful tool in your journey of life. Read it today and, before you know it, you'll be driving yourself happy!

Richard Carlson
January, 2000
Benicia, California

iv

TABLE OF CONTENTS

PART ONE:
Lessons Learned Along The Way

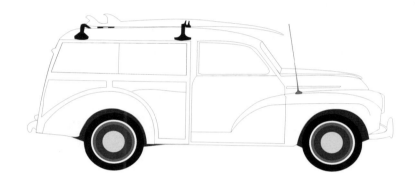

Dedication

To my parents:

THANK YOU DAD, MY 'CAR GUY,' FOR YOUR GIFT OF LOVE and your simple lessons about life shared through your passion for cars.

Thank you mom, for your gift of resilience, humor, integrity, and tenacity. It is you who taught me the final lesson about the value of the precious present moment.

Together you gave your combined wisdom and insights about life from the depth of your heart genuinely and in the ways that you could. I have benefited not only from all that you have given me, but also from all that you could not. Your successes as well as your shortcomings gave me the gift of being able to clearly discern what is important to me.

You taught me how to drive, not only a car, but also my life.

ix

Acknowledgements

Gratitudes

THANK YOU CARRIE AND DANA, for choosing me as your mom. My relationship with you is my greatest treasure. You have taught me the truest meaning of unconditional love, loyalty, humor, forgiveness, and acceptance. You are incredible women, inside and out. How blessed we are to have one another.

Thank you, dear friend Richard. You have shared your *Don't Sweat the Small Stuff* journey of success with generosity. You have loved and mentored me through my discouragement and gifted me with your time, talents, and experience. I treasure you as a colleague and friend.

Thank you Debbie, my sister, my friend. I am grateful for your sense of humor, your tenacious strength, your unwavering encouragement, and your limitless belief in me.

Thank you, Richard, for challenging me to live what I believe. You have emphasized for me the importance of my commitment to transforming life from a struggle to a joy ride.

Also, special thanks to Marye Thomas, Marilyn Brazier, Karen Morrell, Karla Morrell, Dr. Grease (Bob Hagin), BBK-TCHR (Carole Hagin), Bus Driver Bill, Timothy D., Duffy and Jane, Tex, Donna and Michael, and Rob and Linda Cook for all of your love, encouragement, patience and support when I was both 'on' and 'off course.' I treasure having you in my cheering section.

Cover design by Michael Blatt, interior design by Courtenay Design Group.

About Your Driving Instructor:
Why Me? Why Happiness?

DEAR FRIENDS AND FELLOW TRAVELERS,

Let's face it. Life is a trip! Maneuvering the road of life with enthusiasm, ease, skill, and wonder is a great adventure that we often perceive as an inconvenient series of problems, one after another. Several years ago I attended a driving school where we were taught basic automobile maintenance and techniques for handling our car in a skid, during a blowout, on curves and amidst unexpected obstacles. Life presents us with similar emotional inconveniences. Having strategies for how to handle the twists and turns of life will prove to be as practical and valuable as knowing how to handle your car with confidence. There is much to learn from the parallels between the two. I am delighted to be your driving instructor for traveling the road of life and offer you a refresher course in how to *DRIVE YOURSELF HAPPY.*

Who is this book for?

While most books are written to address a specific niche, the search for success, joy and meaning in life is not exclusive to a particular audience. Whether you are a business executive, a parent, a caregiver, an employee, a partner—or any person who faces the challenges of being human—you have experienced the impact of accelerated change and relentless stress. I promise this book will be of benefit to you.

Like millions of people, life is driving you crazy. You are probably feeling off course, and struggle to balance your life personally and professionally. You lack enthusiasm as you pull yourself out of bed each morning wondering if you will ever be really happy.

Defining Happiness

What does it mean to be happy?

DON'T YOU THINK IT'S ABOUT TIME TO REDEFINE HAPPINESS? Driven by our false expectations, we cannot be happy until all of the circumstances of our life are handled—our life is in order, everything is working perfectly, our 2.8 kids are grown, have a 3.6 grade point average, we are the perfect weight, our IRA is fully funded, everyone likes us, and we can afford to sit and sip margaritas on some sunny stretch of beach somewhere. It's not a wonder that we loose sleep and sit with varying degrees of disillusionment and fatigue instead, rather than with salt on the rim of our glass.

We set ourselves up for failure. We never reach our intended destination because we impose limitations and conditions on our definition of happiness. What if we discovered that happiness already is? What if we have just blocked our vision or taken a bit of a detour? Happiness is ours now when we clarify our definition, making it more accessible from a new perception.

Contrary to what we are told often, the journey of life is not about getting 'there.' The real truth is that there is no 'there' there. Now is all we really have. Our adventure is about changing our focus. It's about finding our way home by looking inward more than we look outward for what we are looking for. It involves taking the wheel and steering our way back to the main road of moment–to–moment joy. Blending together one conscious moment after another, we realize a deep sense of peace even on the occasions that the road we travel is rough or slippery. We get a glimpse of knowing that the most important things in life aren't things.

What a relief it is when we recognize that happiness need not be limited only to when life is going as we planned. It can exist simultaneously with sadness, change, and disappointment by changing our viewpoint and expanding the way we look at life, placing our attention on now. With an open mind and a willing heart we discover that joy can exist—even amidst detours and less than perfect times. We really can be happy regardless of our circumstances. Trust me, it's possible.

Why should you trust me?

Children in innocence often ask insightful questions. When I was a kid I began to notice the evident number of unhappy people. Everyone seemed too anxious or too busy to experience joy and recognize the things I saw as wonderful about life. My questions of why were never met with a clear answer. It didn't make sense to me. I couldn't understand why people would over–and–over make the choices that had already proved to lead them to greater stress and unhappiness. It didn't seem like it was meant to be that way. Hmmmm, choice. Most of us don't believe that we really have a choice.

This childhood curiosity prompted my attempts as an adult to unravel this mystery. My investigation was channeled into my psychological training and private practice for over twenty years in the field of stress management. Though I was clinically trained as a stress expert, and had plenty of my own stress to prove this true, it only took me fifty years to gather the courage to declare myself an expert in happiness instead.

All my studies, degrees, credentials, and work experience have served me immeasurably; however, they offered me only limited clues and guidelines for how to be happy. They outlined and belabored the severe complexities of unhappiness. Life was not defined as a natural state that was occasionally interrupted by a painful experience. Instead, the pain of life was the expected state that was occasionally relieved by moments of joy. Of course, happiness caused suspicion and was criticized as a way of avoiding 'real' issues.

The focus was on the negative, and the message was that life is hard. The conclusion is that mental and emotional health is inaccessible or arduous to achieve. It is an involved pursuit for which we just don't have time. So why bother?

Without a doubt there are serious psychological disorders that require more than the strategies offered in this book. However, most of us are fortunate enough to enjoy basic emotional stability. All we need are specific directions for how to calm our negative thinking and and change our focus from the things in life that aren't working. We need a cheering section to applaud us as we redirect our energy to all the things that are working. Despite our fears, we are not broken. From time to time we forget that we are essentially magnificent. Happiness is ours when we remember our wholeness, and consciously channel our attention from chaos to calm.

It feels like a bold step at this point in my life to make happiness a priority and teaching happiness my career choice. Many are still focused on dysfunction and use the degree of struggle as their measurement device for success. Effortful living has been our identity for far too long. It's time to head in a new direction.

The key is to be willing.

Has life been driving you crazy? We regard ourselves as victims of life—we whine, complain and blame, unclear how to do it any other way. Most of us would prefer not to see ourselves as victims of life even though we react as if we are at the mercy of it. Setting our fears and disillusionment aside, I believe people are really willing and hungry for relief from the pain of their victimization and negative perception NOW. We all long for a more peaceful, balanced, and meaningful life. Although a bit road weary, we're compelled to make an authentic contribution. We're eager to renew our hope and motivated to learn the practice of living with joy by climbing back in the driver's seat on the journey of life. But, how?

Life is not always easy, but it can be simple even when things are tough. The key is to be willing—letting go of resistance, analysis paralysis, and the need to be right. Life is hard when we feel lost and focus on what's not working. It becomes simple even when it's not easy when we have a clear direction and place our attention on the things that are working. The road is smoother when we muster the courage to take a small step while daring to make the mistakes necessary for our growth. With willingness, love and support the door of limitless possibilities is wide open. We have the ability to remember our wholeness, see our strength, and find our way back to our state of natural joy.

Perfection is not a prerequisite for joy.

To declare expertise in the art of being happy is not meant to imply that we experience unwavering high moods and uninterrupted joy. Contrary to another common myth, perfection is not a prerequisite for joy. Let me be the first to admit that I have moments when I let the circumstances of life get the better of me, causing me to feel totally isolated from my wisdom, compassion, creativity, and confidence. Like almost everyone, I occasionally experience a melt down. I have my fair share of heartbreak, mistakes, and emotional baggage to declare. The reassuring news, even though we resist it, is that setbacks are an integral part of teaching us what we are here to learn to expand our success and personal excellence. We all have them. Living a purposeful life of self–acceptance is what life is all about.

Even with and expanded by life's inevitable highs and lows I consider myself to be a happy person. It is because I have detoured into sadness and disillusionment that I have become a more credible guide. Because I steadfastly hold joy and simplicity as my compass even when at the bottom of one of life's potholes, I can offer you a personally tested road map to more consistent happiness regardless of your circumstances. I can also offer you the assurance based on experience that you will be all the stronger for your off–road experience.

None of us look forward to periods of great effort and challenge. Many of us have perfected avoidance and denial. Over time and with patience, though, I have learned the benefits of embracing rough times rather than resisting them. Like it or not, there is always a valuable lesson and all things have a deeper significance.

There is always a gift. When we are open to this, all facets of life become easier. We can welcome and integrate them to our benefit. Our self–confidence expands when we willingly face each situation with courage and curiosity, rather than fighting or sidestepping life's obstacles immobilized by our fears and consumed by doubt.

Happiness as a priority.
Happiness is easily discounted as a subject of substantial value in face of serious corporate decisions or the world's social problems. Yet, we no longer can ignore the impact of the increasing number of people disconnected from their joy. Unhappiness continues to be dramatically demonstrated by fits of road rage, school shootings, job dissatisfaction, domestic violence, drug and alcohol abuse, and other social symptoms of pain and despair. It may seem too simplistic, but it is our disconnection from happiness that feeds the problems we face.

Estranged from true happiness, we are suspicious of and even irritated with anyone who seems content with life. Perhaps they are in denial, on drugs, or wanting to sell us something. We conclude that if they are smiling they're up to no good. Our suspicion disguises our true jealousy. We feel that if we cannot be happy, no one can! What we really wish is that we had their sense of optimism. Instead, we resign ourselves to feeling alone.

To fill our emptiness we seek out those who will commiserate, taking odd delight in the competition of seeing whose life is more complex. As the saying goes, "Misery loves company."

Fear has a loud voice when it raises doubt in the strength of love and the power of happiness.

What if…"Fear knocked at the door. Faith answered. No one was there." —*Old English Proverb*

The pain of the world has been enough to lull us into resignation. We need to shift our focus away from what is not working and retrain our attention on how good it will be to live in a world where happiness is operating at full capacity. We must then move step–by–step in that direction with relentless and resilient conviction.

I have chosen happiness as my priority. I invite you to do the same and see what miracles happen. It is because happiness is my direction even though I fall off course from time to time that I regard myself as a trustworthy driving instructor for your refresher course in learning how to *DRIVE YOURSELF HAPPY*.

Life on the road to happiness.

My commitment is to teach about happiness until those who have forgotten remember that we are already whole and complete. It will remain my purpose until we all can rest in self–acceptance, greater consciousness, and dare to love others and ourselves to full capacity. All of us will experience a better world when we are certain of our unique gifts without being distracted by self–doubt.

The "C" word.

Many of us have developed an allergic reaction to commitment. We regard it as something irreversible, restrictive and painful as a result of our own distorted experiences of the truth. But, it's gotten a bum rap. Commitment is a promise to willingly remain conscious about having our words and actions match our values, to admit and amend when we fall short, and to renegotiate with integrity when we must. It invites us to be who we really are. That's a good thing.

One of the 'funny' things about life is that when we make a commitment to something specific, we can expect any number of opportunities to test our level of commitment. The publication of this book has been a lengthy process, and I honestly considered giving up more than once. I questioned at each apparent roadblock if it might be too big a dream to create a way for happiness to be believable and applicable for those who are weary from their travels.

Every strategy and belief has been tested. Self–doubt crept in, hooked up cable and ordered pizza more than once. Somehow finding the energy when I thought there was none left, doing my best to 'walk my talk', and having the encouragement to start one more time than I stopped is what finally brought this book across the finish line.

I sincerely hope this book will be one of those treasured resources on your shelf that you visit often, as you would a dear friend. However, I did not write this book only for you. I wrote this book as a handy reference guide for myself, as well, to remind me of the things that are truly important. Like you, I will reach for it when I need a reminder of the wisdom I know, but have forgotten. It will assist me in redirecting myself back to the road of happiness, helping me remember that love is what fuels the adventure we face.

I offer you within the covers of this book some simple directions for maneuvering more happily through life, making it possible for us to fully experience each day—each life of days—as a little more satisfying and simple, regardless of our circumstances.

So, how do we realign with happiness?

How do we create simple ways to remember our commitment, day–in and day–out, to a life of joy when we are tested and tempted to forget? How do we shift from apathy to anticipation? From fear to excitement? From criticism to compassion? From sarcasm to hope? How do we find the courage to prioritize what is important to us and dare to live boldly according to what we believe? That's what this book, this adventure, is all about.

There is no magic formula. There are many variables and unknowns. The journey is more fun when we venture along this road of discovery with a flexible sense of where we are going, willing to make mistakes and open to learning from them. When we travel with love as our ultimate goal we refocus our perceptions. Gradually we decipher a more efficient and enjoyable way of life that is more than just making a living. This new awareness provides us with the ability to recognize the signs of happiness along the way that affirm what we have known all along—that love is always the answer, being happy is a choice, and both are possible regardless of our circumstances.

Please pause and linger long enough with your renewed wisdom to see new possibilities well after the pages of this book are closed. If so, I will have done what I came to do.

Fasten your seat belt, put your hands on the wheel, welcome aboard, and remember to…

Travel lighthearted,

Rhonda Hull

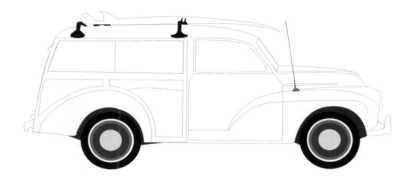

New Road Rules for the Human Race:
Why You? Why Cars?

THE ALARM GOES OFF IN THE MORNING. Before our eyes are open our mind starts spinning. We compete for the bathroom, are cut off from the last cup of coffee, grumble as we race to the front door maneuvering through the household obstacle course. Finally, we're out of the house and ready to make a pit stop at our local coffee house looking for a caffeine jump–start.

Are you caught up in feeling like life is a race, not a journey? Despite your efforts, you still seem to hit every personal road-block and professional pothole. As hard as you try to balance being all things to all people, you experience that the expectations of work and family mix about as well as oil and water.

LIFE IN THE FAST LANE

There is no escaping it. Life moves in the fast lane these days expecting us to process in one day the same amount of information that our grandparents processed over a two–year period of time. It seems like an insurmountable task to drive ourselves happy when we feel like we are on a collision course with stress. Our solution? Rather than slow down, we go faster and go numb.

It is hard to slow down when we have come to believe that four hours of sleep a night is generous, antacids are appetizers and a sixty–plus hour workweek is to be expected. Stress has become our loyal companion. So loyal that it often lasts longer than many marriages—and evidently with a stronger commitment to the vow, "until death do us part." What starts out as impatience, sleepless nights, and panic attacks expands into an endless litany of stress related illnesses. Day–after–day, mile–after–mile, we think 'if' only we resolve our circumstance, 'then' we will eliminate our stress and have the time to be happy. Have you noticed that no matter how fast you go, there is always more to do? There has got to be a better way!

Is life a joy ride or destruction derby

The human race need not be an endurance race any longer. The good news is that happiness is contagious. Just listen to a baby laugh! It is time for us to apply new road rules so life can become a joy ride rather than remain a destruction derby.

If you are still holding this book, it tells me you believe there could be a different avenue to happiness and that you are open to discovering what it could be. Given the accelerated speed of the world today you probably don't think you have the time to learn new strategies for happier and more successful living. It is understandable that you are skeptical of promises of easy relief and resistant to one more demand on your time.

Roadside assistance

DRIVE YOURSELF HAPPY contains roadside assistance even for those who are traveling life at hyper–speed. Open the book anywhere with only a minute to spare, or read it cover to cover, over and over whenever you have more time. As if by magic, there will always be the ideal tidbit of wisdom waiting for you at just the right time. At literally every turn you will find how best to adjust your course to access your natural state of joy.

Even if a devoted pedestrian, the automobile has become an American icon to which all can relate. Symbolically, we can see the correlation of our body as a car and our soul as the engine. Together they represent a metaphoric 'vehicle' by which we maneuver life's highway. The question is, "Who will drive?"

The delightful stories and workable wisdom in this book offer important alterations in our thinking to make our adventure more meaningful, memorable, and magical. Using automobile analogies, *motor–vational* metaphors, and new road signs we find the way to focus on happiness rather than hassle, and to be reminded of our wisdom when we forget. In so doing we discover that it really is possible to be happy regardless of our circumstances.

Stop to consider what it would be like to live in a world where people were content and you could work surrounded by truly happy people? Not just 'fair weather' happiness dependent on getting a better job, making more money, moving to a bigger home, or getting a sexy new partner—but people happy from the inside out. Imagine what it would be like if everyone was committed to personal and professional balance, willing to put first things first and have their words and actions match? Rather than get distracted convincing everyone else of the benefits of happiness, why not start with you?

Becoming your own mechanic

Although at times it is necessary to take your car to a specialist, you can save time and money by gaining a clear understanding of how your car works and expand your ability to do some of the everyday maintenance yourself. *DRIVE YOURSELF HAPPY* provides some tools necessary for an attitude adjustment. It teaches you how to become your own mechanic and inspires you to climb back into the driver's seat of your own life, leaving the role of victim in the dust.

DRIVE YOURSELF HAPPY is ideal for busy people, because being happy it is a moment–by–moment adventure where leaps of faith are optional. Life is a process where small but persistent increments of change can be as effective as huge strides forward. Often they prove to be more durable. Every step, big or small, is progress and worth celebrating.

Confucius, the famous philosopher once said, "A journey of a thousand miles begins when you start your engine"—or maybe it was "with a single step."

Change does not require huge steps. It often only requires a minimum investment of time and a greater investment of willingness, dispelling the myth that 'bigger is better.' Whatever size step we take, what is most important is that it be purposeful. Even 'baby steps' take you further on the road of success.

But I just don't have time.

Have you ever been late for an appointment thinking you didn't have time to stop for gas only to sputter, cough, and run out along the way? You spend three times as much time cursing at the side of the freeway waiting for help than it would have taken to 'fill up.' We operate by the myth that speed is a requirement for success and efficiency. We believe we have to go faster and faster. The truth is, if we don't stop to refuel and reconsider our course of action we will eventually get nowhere fast and be no further ahead.

We think it will take a miracle in our busy schedule to learn to apply new strategies. The good news is that miracles are time efficient. They are a shift in perception that can happen in an instant when we are willing. In slowing down and opening our mind, we actually can go faster, and with greater clarity, productivity and joy.

By avoiding intimidating psychobabble and applying practical concepts, *DRIVE YOURSELF HAPPY* promises to be a fun continuous read for a full tune–up. It is also suitable for short pit stops when you need quick fixes along the way. When learning to drive, whether in a car or on the journey of life, theory plus a bit of 'behind the wheel' application give you the optimum opportunity to acquire stronger maneuvering skills. Some prefer learning theory before grabbing the wheel. Others learn best with direct and immediate hands–on experience. Depending on your personality and learning style and the time you have amidst your busy day, there is something here for everyone.

WHAT'S IN THE ROAD AHEAD?

DRIVE YOURSELF HAPPY is made up of two parts to make the information in this book more easily accessible.

PART ONE offers brief stories and insights that convey *DRIVE YOURSELF HAPPY* concepts, humor and wisdom.

PART TWO offers *DRIVE YOURSELF HAPPY* redefined road signs, practical suggestions for their application, and 'behind the wheel' exercises as memorable guidelines for happier living.

Using these road signs combined with *motor–vational* metaphors and automobile analogies, *DRIVE YOURSELF HAPPY* promises to:

- Put spark back in your plugs by renewing your creativity personally and professionally
- Recharge your battery by increasing your energy level and sense of self worth
- Refuel your tank to give you greater decision making power
- Fine tune your engine by strengthening your intuition, clarity, and inner wisdom
- Balance your tires spiritually, physically, mentally and emotionally to increase your resilience and compassion
- Get your life on course while welcoming mistakes as an opportunity to learn, using your values as your road map
- Shift your perception and expand your ability to experience happiness regardless of your circumstances
- Tune you into the power of PMS (Present Moment Seeing)

Breathe deep, be willing and open your heart to enjoy the journey.

PART ONE

LESSONS LEARNED ALONG THE WAY

CHAPTER ONE

SCENIC ROUTE

SCENIC ROUTE

*Learn to look for signs of happiness
and accept that life is a trip.
It is a moment–by–moment trip.
Why not enjoy it?*

NO ONE IS IMMUNE. I was having one of those days. I was running late and caught in traffic along with what seemed like half the world's population. We were all crammed on the same stretch of highway. Our commute became a serious competition for the same extra car length of pavement. We act as if arriving seven or eight feet sooner would make the difference. I had 'motor–mind.' My thoughts raced as I was cut off right and left in the bumper–to–bumper steady stream of taillights.

In my more conscious and centered moments I know that I am not a victim and the circumstances of life do not control me unless I let them. When empowered with this clear perception, I know I have a choice about the direction and quality of my life. However, when gritting my teeth and overcome by my old habits of destructive thinking, my life—like the traffic—feels like it is in gridlock.

Trapped not just by the parade of cars, but also by my ability to see only the limited and drama–infested version of my life, I longed for relief and wanted a 'sign.' I was road weary from facing a few of life's challenges. I was also dealing with the recent loss of both of my parents that had been hastened by stress related illnesses. Pain, fatigue and grief were the fuel mixture that sparked my reactions and somehow justified at the time my impatient line of questioning, "What now? What next? Where do I go from here? What am I to do when so alone and lost?"

I had veered off course, felt stuck, and was unsure which way to turn personally or professionally. I prayed for—no, I

1

demanded a clearer sense of direction. I hoped a miracle would free me from driving in circles and allow me to loosen my grip on the worry wheel of my out of control life.

BLIND SPOTS.

We all have them. Our blind spots are triggered by unrealistic expectations, disappointment, and loss. Sadly, and all too often, they obscure our inner wisdom and rob us of the access to our serenity and peace of mind.

Limited sight impairs our ability to recognize the answers, lessons, and solutions that are otherwise so obvious. Paralyzed by our fear, we backtrack in reverse and get stuck in the past. Our wheels spin without traction reliving our misfortunes. We overlook opportunities to adjust our course and bypass chances to head in a better direction.

This time, though, it was different. I experienced one of those 'ah–ha' moments when the fog finally lifted. Driving along in traffic feeling sorry for myself, I noticed as if for the first time a road sign I had probably seen millions of times before: ADOPT–A–HIGHWAY. According to the vehicle code handbook this sign is posted along the roadway to acknowledge the community group or business that takes on the expense and responsibility of keeping that particular stretch of highway free of litter, and reminds us to do our part.

The familiar road sign that I had seen over and over on my daily travels all of a sudden took on a new and deeper meaning. Distracted by my expectation that the answer would come in a different form I almost missed it being right there before my eyes. The ADOPT–A–HIGHWAY road sign no longer was just a reminder to keep the roadway free of litter. It transformed into an inescapable, repetitive and easily accessible reminder posted everywhere for my benefit. Durable happiness is mine when I ADOPT–A–HIGHWAY—adopt a higher way of thinking, adopt a different perspective that embraces the power of love and the value of present moment seeing.

COULD IT BE THAT SIMPLE?

Could these road signs be the 'sign' for which I was looking? Could they offer obvious and available solutions for remembering the wisdom we already know, but so easily forget? With this simple moment of insight I experienced a relief similar to that of remembering where I had left my car keys, thinking them lost. New vision and greater willingness allowed me to recognize that the answer I was asking for had always been right before my eyes. It was not that happiness had been gone. It was that I had been unable to see it—until now.

My drive that day changed my personal life and focused my professional purpose. I found not only ADOPT–A–HIGH-WAY, but every 'sign' along the way carried a subliminal message that offers a refresher course in happiness.

LIFE IS ONLY SIXTEEN INCHES.

The journey of life may seem long when calculated in years, but short when calculated in inches. Believe it or not the journey of life is only about sixteen inches. How can that be? It is because the journey is from our head to our heart. Although a short distance, it provides an incredible path of unfolding adventure for those who dare to see from a refreshed perspective.

These newly defined 'signs of happiness' become welcome traveling companions as we remember to keep our face to the sun. Happiness in not a place at which we arrive. It is a moment–by–moment method of traveling.

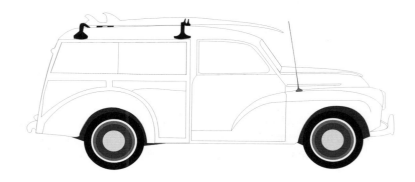

CHAPTER TWO

U–TURN
You turn your life around,
no one else can. Don't wait.
Trust your magnificence now
and step into the driver's seat.

ALMOST EVERYTHING I EVER NEEDED TO KNOW ABOUT LIFE, I learned from a "car guy." Perhaps a car enthusiast seems like an unlikely mentor for life's lessons until you realize this teacher was my father. He had a passion for classic automobiles—driving them, fixing them and collecting them. He was the first to admit he was not perfect. He considered himself a simple man who admitted his share of mistakes, but always with a tender heart and genuine humility. At times by what he did successfully, and as often by the ways he fell short of his good intentions, he offered me crucial and sustaining guidance for joyful and confident living.

My dad's efforts, enthusiasm, and presence of being are crystallized into basic rules for the road of life and now provide me with a map for easier travel. By daring to fail as well as daring to succeed he inspired my strategies for happiness and made me profoundly conscious of the importance of present moment seeing.

My dad worked hard and had tremendous strength even though he had broken his back during his teens. Contrary to the prognosis of limitations he was given at that time, he never let it stop him. A litany of diverse jobs led him from Kansas to California where he met, and two weeks later, married my mom with 'no more than ten bucks and a bag of apples.' Eventually they started an insulation business together and both worked long and hard hours driven by the desire to give their daughters more material advantages than they had when growing up with the residue effects of the Depression.

Work never afforded them much free time, but with high hopes, my dad bought a motorhome and dreamed of traveling across the country someday. 'Someday' never came, at least not fast enough when work always seemed more important. Sadly, the only time he really got to use his motor home was with the decline of my parent's health. They used it to travel to and from the hospital parking lot. It provided familiar over–night shelter when they stood loyal vigil for one another through surgeries, procedures and heart attacks.

DON'T WAIT TO BE HAPPY

My dad died in 1992. Postponing happiness became a sad part of his legacy and an important part of his message that lives on today. Through his profound sacrifices of work imbalance, limited well–being and ill health, he offers a vivid warning of the consequences of stress. His life and his passing compel us with certainty to know that there is a price to be paid by waiting to choose joy.

Our 'in–basket' continues to regenerate long after our energy and health don't. By waiting as if he had forever to take time to renew and enjoy himself, my dad missed many opportunities to be here now. Through this ironic 'gift of opposites'—not taking time for himself—he was the one who taught me that now is the only moment you really have. Happiness is not finally a fulfilled pursuit at the end of the road. It is the enjoyment of the simple pleasures available along the way. His life reminds us to embrace happiness now. His death reminds us not to wait.

My dad's spirit is still very present with me. He was a big man not only in stature, but also in his degree of integrity. He was surprisingly shy and private. He seldom asked for help and took greater delight in providing it for others. He had hands the size of baseball mitts, and yet it seemed he could fix just about any car with the skill of a surgeon in the dark with a piece of bailing wire as his only tool. Fortunately, I often got to be the surgical assistant holding the flashlight for these occasional after dark mechanical operations.

Do you speak 'car'

From the time I was small, and when traditional words failed, the semantics and experiences that surrounded his love for cars became our bridge of mutual understanding. The language of cars was the avenue through which my father subtly taught me life's valuable lessons—cooperation, independence, how to problem solve, how to be patient and how to observe. I feel fortunate that he somehow gave me permission to question. It was his soft–spoken tolerance that allowed me to grow from my mistakes with the confidence that forgiveness was given freely.

This quiet 'car guy' was a man of few words, but when he spoke, you listened. What he said mattered. There was seldom a thought of crossing him even though he was totally gentle and unassuming. My dad had a signature sense of humor. When he laughed his entire body participated. Uncommon to find in today's world, his word was his bond. Deals were sealed on his handshake—and quite a handshake it was. His huge hand offered a gesture of faith far more dependable than any contract signed in triplicate today.

Though I questioned at times that my dad really understood my introspective feminine nature, I knew without a doubt that he always loved me.

Who would cross the finish line first

As the daughter of a 'car guy,' his mechanical influence was a guiding force from the moment I was born. My birth happened long before fathers were welcomed into the delivery room. Instead, he passed his time awaiting my arrival running back and forth from the waiting room to listen to the Indianapolis 500 auto races on his car radio. The race was over hours before I crossed the finish line, and he always teased me about the dead battery in his car.

With no boys in the family I feel fortunate that I was encouraged to stretch beyond the gender stereotypes to enjoy both 'boy' and 'girl' activities. Although I played with dolls, at age four my dad built us a motorized car that was 'fully loaded' with functional headlights, a keyed ignition, and it's own garage attached to the playhouse in our back yard. By nine I would back the family car up and down the driveway. This was the reward for being the first ready for school every morning. A special father–daughter event was attending the Friday night stock car races or destruction derby. By twelve I had a dirt bike and chased rabbits in the desert. Because of these opportunities I had accrued self–confidence and plenty of miles of behind the wheel experience before the ink was ever dry on my legal driver's license.

The power of the car connection

The car connection with my dad did not end when I left home. Not a phone call from him went by without the opening words, "How's your car running?" At face value it was a conversational question of minimal significance, but when I learned the value in listening to the meaning beneath his words I heard so much more. What a gift it was when I came to understand it was his indirect and disguised way of saying "I love you"—to let me know he cared when more direct words were uncomfortable for him.

If I had based my happiness on waiting to hear specific words with clearer sentiment from my dad I would have missed knowing the depth of his love for me. Learning to hear what he intended to say and developing a willingness to listen with greater acceptance has become a valuable skill that I now know leads to expanded intimacy. Words with congruent actions allow communication on a much deeper level and are far less confined by the limits of Webster.

Not until after my father was gone did I fully appreciate the invaluable wisdom and powerful life lessons this 'car guy' offered me through our conversations laced with auto language and metaphors. How I wish he were still here. How I wish I

8

could hear his belly–laugh, see him in his mechanics coveralls, hold his flashlight, watch him dunk his toast in hot chocolate at midnight, and hear the way he would signal his own arrival by jiggling the change and keys in his pocket.

And, yet he is here, just transformed. His simple love and metaphoric lessons about life live on in ways that are easy to remember. His gift of common sense wisdom blended with my training, experience and insights are here in *DRIVE YOUR-SELF HAPPY*.

Offering an unlikely outline for a more meaningful journey through life, his uncomplicated spirit continues to fuel my passion for my work and blesses me with a sense of purposeful direction. My dad would be most pleased to know that the insights of his life, including its failures and its successes, make a difference not only for me, but also for you by enabling us to fully live each moment noticing signs of happiness on our journey through life in the ways that he could not.

CHAPTER THREE

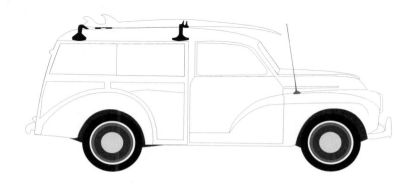

SLOW—CHILDREN PLAYING

Life is a joy ride!
It's the journey from head to heart.
Dare to drive in—into your heart.
It's what's under the hood that counts.

As A CHILD, A ROAD TRIP IN THE CAR SEEMED LIKE IT TOOK FOREVER. Even though sometimes time moved at a slow pace, a car ride was more often a joyous adventure full of wonder. It generated a sense of purpose, a feeling of belonging, and a heightened awareness of simple details. The hours on the road opened the doors to creativity, free flow thinking, and simplicity. To pass the time there was playfulness and laughter. There were sights to be marveled at, wind to dance through your fingers, and alphabet games improvised from license plates and passing signs.

Instead of being an annoyance, traffic jams were an opportunity to make funny faces at those in neighboring vehicles and to hope they would delight us in return with their own. Even confined squabbles with siblings had their benefits, forcing confrontation, resolution, or intervention.

Overhearing parental conversations brought insights and the invitation to stretch our perspective. Falling asleep in the car to the hum of the engine with the warmth of the sun on our faces provided distraction, renewal, comfort and peace. The desire to get to our destination taught us how to ask without demanding and gave us lessons of patience. The wind in our faces made us feel alive, while viewing the passing world through a clean windshield gave us a sense of clarity as well as protection.

Each stop held new possibilities. The destination was usually as fascinating as the journey. And there was comfort in the knowledge that the journey ultimately always took us home again, richer for the adventure.

The journey of life as an adult need be no different. Yet, we have become so removed from such childlike wonder that we have forgotten the source of feeling such happiness is from the inside out. Instead we exhaust our energy chasing after it somewhere out there beyond our grasp. Like a mirage on the horizon, by looking outside ourselves for happiness we don't understand why it continues to elude us.

A detour from delight

Rather than the constant feeling of delight and playfulness that we knew as a child, we are filled with pressure and turmoil. Our enthusiasm, creativity, and sense of humor are overtaken by exhaustion and high–speed worry as we misperceive our circumstances to be the origin of our problems. Not recognizing that we play a part, we're quick to blame one another for our emotional traffic jam. How different this approach is from the child who waves gleefully at total strangers in passing cars expecting joy.

Heart matters

When I was a teenager, I had a friend, Randy, who lived down the street. His car was his world, and his every free moment was spent washing and waxing his vehicle. There had to be at least a hundred layers of wax on that car to create its mirror like finish.

Often when my dad and I would drive together past his house we would observe Randy's car detailing ritual. "You know, you never see the hood up on that car!" my dad would say in his matter–of–fact way. His wise subliminal message wrapped in his metaphoric commentary continued. "It may look great when it's washed and waxed, but a car will still run when the outside's dirty. It will still get you where you need to go. It's great to have a clean car, but always remember," he would advise, "it's what's under the hood that counts."

The journey of life becomes arduous and the destination

seems unattainable when we look for happiness outside of ourselves, thinking it is dependent on what we have or what we look like, rather than based upon who we are. Our authentic worth lies in who we are, not what we do. Our value is intrinsic, not contingent upon our exterior shine. On the surface, perhaps they were just passing comments, but my father's deeper message was that happiness is an inside job.

Why do we so resist the journey from our head to our heart? Our old dysfunctional habit of seeing happiness as something outside of us causes us to experience the journey as something more difficult than it really is.

Drive–in

Traveling inside, softening our expectations for immediate gratification, surrendering our judgments, and letting go of our insistence that life unfold on our terms is what will open our perspective to other possibilities. It allows our experience of life to return to a more genuine and fulfilling form. With insight, innocence and a new way of seeing, life is no longer a task to be endured, but it returns to an adventure to be enjoyed. Enriched rather than enraged by the challenge and change inherent in life, we realize that the most dependable and durable way to return to a sense of child–like wonder is to fully experience every moment along our journey with our willing face to the sun and our heart open to seeing life's magic.

Like the force of a stone at its entry point into water, the power of the wake travels from the center out. It is misguided to think that only when we manage all of the circumstances and control all of the obstacles outside of us will we find happiness. When we acknowledge our own inner worth and nurture 'what's under the hood,' our force will ripple outward and we will tap into the true essence of durable happiness.

Everything is possible in a life of present moments. The choice is ours to make our adult travels as worthwhile as they were when we were children. Now is the perfect time to declare your course of action. Now is the time to embrace life as an incredible journey. Now, as an adult, we get to be the driver and steer the car where we want.

So, take your foot off the brake, choose your direction, and put your life in gear. Ladies and gentlemen, start your engines.

CHAPTER FOUR

TOLL CROSSING

Sometimes life takes its toll.
You're never as alone as you think.
Share your journey
By giving and receiving with grace.

EXACTLY WHEN IS THE COMMUTE HOUR? In the fast pace of today's world, traffic is no longer restricted to a specific few hours a day. The highway seems thick with cars no matter what time it is, day or night. I can't help but wonder where all those people could possibly be going at 3:00 a.m.

Millions and millions of people each day make their way getting to and from 'wherever' on our multi–lane highways. We creep side by side for hours barely daring to glance at one another unless necessary. We are cautious not to maintain eye contact for fear of inciting an outburst of road rage. Constant vigilance and defensiveness amplifies our fatigue and leaves us feeling absurdly alone. In this environment, traveling is no longer fun.

All alone?

Imagine yourself in that commuter caravan of cars moving at a snail's pace. Out of the corner of your eye you notice the driver next to you signaling with one finger. Appalled and ready to react, you first think it's an obscene gesture. With your turn to creep forward twelve non–stop inches, you find relief in confirming that this person is not irreverently motioning to you as you'd first thought. Rocking forward and backward inch by inch, you can't help but notice this person again. Now you realize that he is indeed not extending his middle finger, but his index finger instead. Attempting to understand the purpose of his gesture, you think it is perhaps a friendly warning that a police car is close by. You scan your surroundings and look instinctively through the eyes in the back of your head. Still, no speed trap or red blinking lights to be found.

Then the unthinkable happens. You finally get an all too clear view of what's really happening within the parallel car. With his index finger in a determined motion and oblivious to the slow moving stream of vehicles full of humanity that surround his car on all sides, this person makes his move. Completely self–absorbed and without hesitation, though surrounded by glass, he inserts his index finger into his nostril and uses it with experienced efficiency to probe deeply into his cranial cavity. As if secluded in the privacy of his own home, he accesses what is guaranteed to be a very large piece of mucous matter lodged somewhere around his brain. It's one of the few times you're grateful to be cut off and passed on the highway by a person eager to get somewhere one car length before you.

Gross, you might say? Of course, *we* would never do anything like that. We always maintain the utmost of social etiquette when in our car, even if the 'oldies' tunes happen to be playing on the radio. It makes me wonder. How can we feel so alone and separate as we maneuver through life with six billion or so other people?

BOUNDARIES

When I was a small child I remember visiting the state line area between Nevada and California. As we walked down the sidewalk my dad brought to my attention that we had just passed from one state and now were in another. He continued strolling ahead, but I stopped dead in my tracks and searched the ground as if I had lost something. My dad noticed I had strayed from his side and turned to ask me what I was looking for. "The dotted lines," I replied emphatically, as if it were a silly question. "Where are the dotted lines between the states like on the map at home?"

In my innocence I expected to see real boundary markers on the ground between Nevada and California just as they appear on any map! I was amazed to learn that the boundaries between states or people need not be walls or dotted lines. They are usually permeable imaginary lines where we consciously choose to cross between one place and another— between one person and another.

In our perpetual busy–ness we assume the boundaries between us should be walls. We isolate ourselves seeking refuge behind an amazing illusionary barrier of protection offered by the invisible partition between 'us' and 'them.' We fear we might be hurt. In our attempt to flee our fear, we actually wall it in with us. Unintentionally, we cut ourselves off from feeling the genuine love and compassion that is easily available to us when we trust, and expand our willingness to recognize and receive it.

Acting like a DIP

Have you ever seen the road sign DIP that forewarns a low spot in the road? Using this sign as a conscious reminder that we can choose happiness, we acknowledge that occasionally we isolate ourselves in the low spot by acting like a DIP—a **D**ysfunctionally **I**ndependent **P**erson. When we view our world from such a depressed spot, we experience just that; a depression. Viewing life through a roadblock of exaggerated independence causes us to perceive ourselves as isolated and alone, not realizing it is self–generated. From our distorted vantage point we are less able to see our progress, know we are loved, and remember the truth about our innocence and magnificence.

Depression and discontent threaten happiness at epidemic proportions in our busy world. Some of us feel down. Operating on fumes, we still manage to keep a false smile on our face even though we're completely disconnected from life and who we really are. Isolation is misinterpreted as healthy independence. **D**ysfunctionally **I**ndependent **P**eople often use their obsessive self–sufficiency to disguise their fears and insecurities, never asking for help.

When submerged in over–independence we don't fully realize that we need help. We remain isolated and focus on our destination with a blinding sense of urgency and stubbornness. We think we can't afford the time to refuel or, heaven forbid, ask for directions.

Consumed and distracted by our own circumstances, we fail to appreciate the value of those who are elbow–to–elbow and bumper–to–bumper beside us facing the same perplexities of life that we do. Instead of seeing these fellow travelers as allies along the road of life, we limit ourselves by seeing them as irritants with little to offer us. Relief lies in our ability to choose differently. By adopting a higher vantage point nothing could be further from the truth. The fact is that each and every one of us is a stress expert and therefore we are mutually valuable resources.

Use the CALL BOX

We are not alone! The 'call box' is right there. Though asking for assistance is often what we least feel like doing when we're experiencing a low spot and are discouraged, it's a crucial time for us to reach out for help and to realize we're not without support.

Receiving and giving is a complete gift exchange. Receiving support is not a selfish act, but becomes a joyful responsibility, and a completion of a circle of generosity. Our willingness to ask for help from another gives them the opportunity to give, and in giving, we both receive. Our request for assistance allows others to reach into their own heart and be of service, causing them to experience their own magnificence as well as ours.

By stretching outside of our own glass box, we become more aware of those traveling close by who might need our help.

Having known despair we recognize it in others and are more compassionate of those who might need a jump–start from us along the way.

When we look beyond our own pain and despair, and distract ourselves by acknowledging another, we often receive the unanticipated gift that puts our own tribulations into perspective. Our hearts feel full when we feel that we have made a difference, even if in a small and simple way. In so doing we redirect ourselves back to the happiness highway.

CHAPTER FIVE

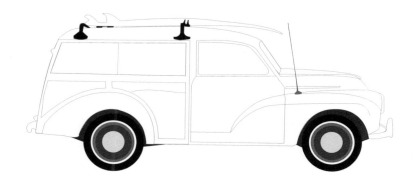

TWO–WAY–TRAFFIC

Dare to discover who you really are.
Be who you are boldly.
Clarify which way you are headed and
invite others to do the same.

EACH NEW CAR COMES WITH AN OWNER'S MANUAL to guide us in its maintenance and servicing care. However, none of us were issued a human version of such a manual when we were born.

We get far more instruction on how to drive a car than we do on how to become happy and fully who we are. Hours of behind the wheel experience are required for a license. We're turned loose with far less preparation to drive through life. Few of us are offered clear guidance to shape our values, and determine our purpose. We have minimal preparation on how to create a healthy relationship, be a loving parent, create genuine success, or deal with disappointments and change. Yet we will encounter all of these on our journey though life.

Although in a marvelous variety of models, shapes and forms, we are all issued the same basic 'vehicle' for our journey through life. We do our best to tailor it and make it uniquely our own. With what we are given, some of us create a life in which we see ourselves as a victim while others recognize that we determine our degree of enjoyment by how we choose to view our circumstances. Depending on whether we react or respond to the circumstances of life, some of us think we've got a lemon while others learn to make lemonade!

PERSONALIZING OUR PATH

Our car is often a telling extension of our personality or a reflection of our life style choices. From personalized license plates and pin striping to promotional antenna balls, leopard dash mats, bumper stickers, a hula girl gyrating on the back dash, or just a special color–coordinated travel mug, we honor and adorn our cars. We even name them as if they were a treasured member of the family. Putting these personal touches on our automobile is one of the few places we dare to disclose any clues about what makes us unique or a hint about who we really are.

My dad would always help me personalize each car I had, usually with a racing stripe or an 'ahooogah' horn. This was the opportunity to declare in a distinct way what made me unique. One day, while together rewiring my horn, it was as if the hood of my car became a temple, and my dad transformed for a moment into a garage guru sharing one of his insights! I remember the gem of a lesson that was to him perhaps only a passing comment. "You know," he said, "it's not what others think of you that matters." After a long pause to contemplate both the wiring and what he would say next, he continued. "It's what you know about who you really are that's important. That's what you want people to remember." Like my dad, I consider myself to be quite shy. Still, he managed to empower me to risk revealing the things that make me my own person in simple, unique, and humble ways.

I think we all want to be acknowledged for the person we really are, accepted unconditionally regardless of our limitations, and recognized for our individual gifts. The thing we desire most in life it to be loved.

As a single mom it took me many years of one class here and another class there before I finally completed my doctorate in psychology. To celebrate my resilience in jumping through the final hoop of the arduous process, my sister Debbie gifted me with a personalized license plate. After my father was gone this gesture reflected a very memorable part of his spirit, so it meant a lot.

IT'S ALL IN HOW YOU SEE IT

The personalized license plate my sister chose for my car in honor of my doctorate in psychology read FMLYPHD—an abbreviation for FAMILY DOCTOR. My degree is in family counseling and developmental psychology so it seemed the fitting celebration of this milestone, and I thought it would be something my dad would have been proud of.

Not long after getting my new plates attached to my car, a gentleman stopped to comment in a parking lot. "I like your license plate." he said. Having misread the plate's meaning, he inquired, "Did you win that car on that game show, *Family Feud*?" At first surprised by his interpretation, I then laughed. I continue to smile every time I consciously notice my license plates. Life is all in how you see it. From that moment on it became hard for me to see my license plate as reading anything else but FAMILY FEUD, instead of FMLYPHD. I knew my dad, with his stellar sense of humor, was having a good chuckle, too.

Human DOing or human BEing

In today's fast paced world, we exaggerate the importance of titles and labels. Have you noticed that when we introduce ourselves, out of social habit we offer our name followed by what we 'do' for a living? We have grown accustomed to having our success judged by our accomplishments. We have come to believe our worth is measured by our capacity to generate a profit, rather than by our ability to demonstrate compassion and generosity without exception. Attention is focused on what we do for a living, rather that on who we are and the courage we employ to discover as best we can how to live a quality life.

Titles, labels and accomplishments give only a limited picture of who we really are, what we love, the meaningful lessons in our life, and what makes us real and authentic. It is an important part of our journey to discover what makes us unique, magnificent and irresistible beyond our accomplishments. It is the spirit, integrity, and courage we implement to accomplish our goals and move beyond our fears that is the truest measure of the quality of our being.

We need not personalize our life in huge ways to feel more alive. It doesn't have to include an adrenaline rush and elevated heart rate. It is often the simple things that best reveal our tenderness and tenacity. The true 'you' can be revealed by remembering to smile for no good reason, or paying for the bridge toll of the person behind you. Release your joy from it's self–imposed restrictions by daring to have dessert first, follow your intuition more often, give a gift anonymously, and write someone a letter on a role of adding machine paper. Be more spontaneous and declare life a joy ride. After all, we are human BEings, not human DOings.

By clarifying and appreciating our true self–worth, we stretch wide our ability to recognize the genuine self–worth of another. With an expanded ability to share mutual unconditional love we learn to be more aware of what the present moment has to offer.

Chapter Six

VISTA POINT
Enjoy P.M.S.
FOCUS ON PRESENT MOMENT SEEING.
EXPAND YOUR ABILITY
TO SEE LIMITLESS POSSIBILITIES.

HAVE YOU EVER DRIVEN IN THE CAR FOR SEVERAL MILES only to realize that you didn't consciously remember the last few miles traveled? This experience far too often mirrors life in general. We have so much on our minds that we are seldom really here in the present moment. Instead, we're either reviewing the past, rehearsing the future, or just plain numb. We're living on adrenaline at the mercy of the expectations of others. All of this robs us of present moment living.

FORGETTING IS FORGIVING

I dare say I am not the only one who finds myself forgetting things more and more often as time marches on. Wisdom and forgetfulness are often traveling companions.

The older I get, the more tempted I am to complain, especially when the natural process of aging is promoted by our culture as something to be resisted. Though the process has been happening for ages and generations to millions and millions, it still seems like a surprise when it happens to us. Our critical voice is always ready to find and focus on evidence for our diminished mobility and increased forget-fulness, particularly when someone's name escapes us or we can't immediately remember where we parked our car. Such moments leave us feeling inadequate, powerless, and distracted from the present moment. We expend our energy being upset, making remembering effortful. When will we learn that acceptance is a better way?

We could all learn a thing or two from my great Aunt Zella.

She is a sweet, kind and gentle lady barely over five feet tall, but a giant in character. I'm certain she could wrestle a bear and win if she had to. Don't let her frail stature fool you. To look at her you would never suspect her tenacity. She lives in Fredonia, Kansas, where I believe the average age is about 80. I think Aunt Zella is now close to 98. This qualifies her as a senior citizen there, but just barely.

Zella is quite a remarkable lady with an incredibly resilient spirit. She still has an admirable recall of the experiences and people of her youth and in–depth details of the blessings and challenges that shaped her past. Although my Great Aunt Zella's present moment memory retention has narrowed over time to about a twenty–minute window of sustainable recollection, she still maintains a unique sense of optimism, acceptance, and wonder.

I make it a point to write Zella at least once a month and my cousin Jean faithfully reads her my letters. She shares with me how much Zella enjoys my correspondence, and, then with candor comments that the nice part is that her mom gets to enjoy them over and over again. You see, Jean can read Aunt Zella my letter in the morning, and by noon she has forgotten that she already heard it, and is just as happy to hear it again. Spread out over twenty minute intervals, my letters bring repetitive delight to Zella, and she responds to each reading as joyfully as if it were the first. I am grateful to know that I contribute to her happiness ten–fold, by the simple act of writing a letter.

SMALL THINGS WITH GREAT LOVE

Genuine happiness often is the result of very simple acts of kindness, and often we do not get to know the full benefits of our seemingly unimportant gestures. It was Mother Teresa who reminded us, "You cannot do great things in this life. You can only do small things with great love."

Even though for her age Aunt Zella is quite spry, I was not

26

surprised by the news from my cousin several months ago that my Aunt Zella had fractured her hip. An injury of this nature is not uncommon for a person of her age. Inquiring how it happened, I was amazed to learn that, true to her nature, Aunt Zella had sustained the injury to her hip falling in her aerobics class! For several weeks Jean would keep me informed about her recovery process. She said that the greatest challenge was to have someone be on hand when Zella would awaken from a nap to prevent her from getting up, for fear she would forget that her hip was broken and be eager to get back to her aerobics class. I am grateful to say that Aunt Zella has fully recovered. She is back to her old antics with a bit more care and at a little slower pace, but with no less passion and exuberance.

It is said that when the student is ready, the teacher appears. Aunt Zella is probably unaware that she has been an invaluable role model for me. Her uncomplicated zest for living got me to thinking about what it would be like to live so fully in the present moment by choice rather than dictated solely by chronology or ill–health.

What would it be like to have life be that fresh, and renewable every twenty minutes? To some degree, I resisted the thought of this mental pause and saw it as a limitation. Now, thanks to Aunt Zella, I began to consider instead that it might be quite wonderful if we all could live that way all the time, with our window for the present moment wide open. The more I considered it might be a potential gift, the more magnificent and peaceful I realized such a reality could be. It meant that even the worst transgression would be forgiven and forgotten in that focused window of present moment living. There in lies true and durable happiness.

WOULD YOU RATHER BE RIGHT OR HAPPY
My dad always said, "The older you get, the faster 'it' goes. I have found this to be true of time and memory. We don't

27

have time to forget to forgive. We need to redefine forgiveness. It does not mean we must condone the actions of another, but find the fortitude and compassion to place the transgression in the past, refocusing on the power of now. By withholding forgiveness to prove a point or make ourselves 'right,' we are the only one who loses a good night's sleep. Ask yourself often, "Would I rather be right or happy?"

When we come to a CATTLE XING sign and a cow is actually standing in the middle of the road, we have to acknowledge it is there before we can take evasive action. The same is true on the road of life when we confront the obstacle of anger and have the opportunity to forgive. Denial, avoidance, and anger insure a 'head on collision' and are certain to bring us pain. Forgiveness is a better choice. It brings freedom, peace, and a smoother ride.

We must not only be willing to forgive others, but forgive ourselves of our shortcomings and limitations as well. It is important to become aware of our negative self–talk and develop a gentler conversation with ourselves. There is a difference between holding ourselves accountable for our actions and 'raking ourselves over the coals.' Guilt is a poor substitute for taking authentic action and accomplishes nothing but keeping us immobilized. Willingly correcting our mistakes with compassion and forgiveness leads to lasting change and a clearer present moment perspective.

Choose to make now a priority by implementing forgiveness. Opening our hearts and expanding our ability to care, opens our window to the happiness of the present moment.

CHAPTER SEVEN

DEER CROSSING
Happiness is dear. Choose kindness.
Life is not a rigorous process
of self–improvement,
but a gentle and forgiving process
of self–acceptance.

MEMORY IS AN AMAZING AND CURIOUS THING. Scientific fact teaches us that our memory is housed in and monitored by a specific part of our brain. Demonstrated through a special procedure, a surgeon can use a probe to stimulate the brain in a certain spot, activating the patient's ability to recall otherwise forgotten memories.

OUR MEMORY MOVED

Although this evidence strongly supports that our memory resides in our cranial cavity, my personal experience seems to challenge this long held belief. Gravity takes its toll not only on our face, chin, thighs and breasts, but also on the location of our memory. Could it be possible that due to the forces of gravity our memory winds up in our rear end?

You might think this a radical alternative theory, but consider this all too common scenario. We are sitting in our special chair listening to music or watching TV. We decide to get up and go into the other room to get our car keys and head off to the store to get a few things for dinner. Prying ourselves from our comfy spot we walk a few feet into another part of the house where our keys are located. Our pace slows. We stop dead in our tracks as we realize midway that our memory has failed us. To save our life we can't remember why we wandered into the adjoining room.

With great aggravation, our self–inquisition begins to assault our self–acceptance. We are irritated with ourselves that in less than twenty feet we have forgotten what we went to retrieve. Incredible frustration sets in and a heated avalanche of counter–productive self–talk begins.

To prompt our recall we desperately employ logical problem solving. We quiz ourselves relentlessly about what we were doing before we got up from our comfortable spot hoping there might be a clue. About ready to blow a head gasket, we dare not admit to others why we are pacing with a furrowed brow and a perplexed look on our face.

Efforting to remember

The effort to remember is like being stuck in a rut spinning our wheels. We press on the accelerator repetitively hoping to gain our freedom. Instead, we create a spray of mud that soon becomes a gigantic hole. This all too common experience demonstrates a classic definition of insanity—to try the same thing over and over expecting a different result.

A sense of humor helps at times like this. We all have done it. In one of our insane moments we get out of the car to survey our situation, then get back in the car and try the same unsuccessful strategy again. We hope that our increased wishful thinking will be enough to change the outcome of our repetitive mind loop. We persist in expecting the results to change without having changed our behavior.

Covered with self–propelled mud we remain stuck in our old way of thinking because we fail to realize that it is our need for control and our fear of lack that shackles us to our old pattern of negative thinking. We limit our progress by our diminished creativity and lack of willingness to open to new possibilities.

Finally, we give up our effort to recall. Still paralyzed in mental constipation, we retreat back to our favorite chair and our remote control in forced surrender. And then it happens! Insight finally comes and we recall our mission. What allows this magical moment of remembering? What turns the key and unlocks a free flow of recollection? How do we finally get free? What allows us to suddenly reconnect with what we couldn't previously remember?

Like magic, as soon as our rear end brushes the edge of our favorite chair our memory is often reactivated. Answers find us more often when we give up our need to manipulate a specific outcome. Clarity is ours when we surrender and put our mind in neutral. When we replace our need to control with a willingness to surrender, the road ahead becomes smoother.

Many of us were taught that happiness comes at a price. We have come to believe that pain and manipulation is the only trustworthy road to success. We have dutifully chosen dis–ease rather than ease. We fear that surrender leads to complacency and 'losing our drive.' Therefore, it seems a ridiculous concept to give up and take the path of least resistance as a more certain route to happiness and prosperity. But, what if it were true?

Letting go and allowing

Remembering the wisdom we know becomes effortless and fun when we do not force a particular outcome, but allow the answers to come to us without racing after them in a full speed chase.

As funny as it sounds, sometimes we have to 'let go' in order to 'have.' To surrender does not mean to give up. It means to have faith and implement trust. To detach does not mean we are indifferent and don't care. It means we care enough to accept what is with grace. It is a self–confident way without all the effort, drama, resistance and struggle of experiencing happiness amidst the unpredictable. It allows the focus of our efforts to find us without struggle—be it your car keys, prosperity, love, or happiness.

As odd as it may seem, letting go is integral to transforming our sense of lack and seeing ourselves as abundant. When we have the courage to let go and to accept that all things happen for a reason, we expand our ability to appreciate what we have, creating greater flow. Giving to give rather than giving to get with heartfelt gratitude greases the wheel of prosperity and eases the flow of traffic.

TUNE IN TO HAPPINESS

Do you remember the old car radios? With a gradual spin of the knob we could adjust our reception and eliminate static in order to get a clear broadcast of our favorite radio station. If we got interference, it did not mean that someone had moved the radio station further away. It meant instead, that the radio station was there, but our reception was blocked. We were merely unable to tune into the correct frequency. So it is with happiness. We think that happiness comes and goes. It remains illusive only when we forget to remember that it already IS.

YOUR INCREDIBLE SELF

So how do we understand the real meaning of happiness? Happiness already IS. Although life is a journey, we need not pursue joy. It is always present and only limited by our willingness and ability to tune into its frequency. The quality of our journey is determined by our relationship with what IS—our Incredible Self. Happiness IS not a result of controlling our environment; happiness IS learning to go with the flow of the circumstances in our life. Enjoy all that already IS.

We are not a passenger or victim of life, but a participating driver. No longer a back seat driver of life, or chauffeured, we are learning how to drive ourselves. *DRIVE YOURSELF HAPPY* is not a self–improvement course that is done to us. It is a process of self–acceptance that we participate in by choice. We know we're back behind the wheel when life is wonderful—even when it doesn't appear to be. We trust that we're incredible even when we don't remember we are.

CHAPTER EIGHT

CONSTRUCTION ZONE

Life is a journey,
not merely a destination.
Change is a part of success.
Welcome, rather than resist it.
Let wonder and patience find you again.

CONSTRUCTION ZONE
EXPECT DELAYS

THERE IS NO 'THERE' THERE. Still we are in such a hurry these days to get wherever 'there' may be that we often don't ever experience being fully right 'here.' Our inquisitive wonder about simple things has been substituted with high tech video games that create virtual reality rather than inspired imagination. Situation comedies on TV leave us expecting a resolution to any problem within its thirty–minute time slot and we're justifiably upset if there isn't. We neglect taking the time to fill up our soul and refuel our spirit and live with anxiety instead.

Today we are driven by a sense of urgency. We demonstrate an unrealistic and frightening sense of entitlement that for an alarming number has led to front–page news. Tolerance, compassion and patience have become an endangered species as we chase after happiness somewhere out there. No wonder we are so stressed! No WONDER.

AH, THE LOST ART OF WONDER

Do your remember going on a Sunday drive as a kid? "How much longer, daddy? I'm tired. I'm hungry. I have to go to the bathroom. Are we there yet, daddy?" The barrage of questions would usually start soon after the car pulled out of the driveway. Childhood impatience is innocent rather than calculated. It is motivated by a child's distorted sense of time combined with an insatiable sense of wonder rather than by a sense of entitlement or aggravation.

The joy of wonder is exaggerated when looking forward to Christmas, a birthday party, or to having a friend spend the night. Do you recall the eager feeling of anticipation of a special date, the excitement of a long awaited family vacation, or the impending arrival of the tooth fairy that made the quarter under the pillow all the more meaningful because of the wait? I can remember spending hours savoring the thoughts of what was to come—savoring the joy of imagining, planning and anticipating. The waiting was bittersweet. And, finally would come the day, the moment, or the experience that provided the exuberant feeling of actually having our dream become a reality. This was equal to and in no way diminished the delight of the preceding period of excitement. Both were incredible. Both were wonder–full...full of wonder.

THE 'IF–THEN' FORMULA FOR HAPPINESS

The greatest quality we can nurture in our children, and remind ourselves of in the process, is the wonder many of us once knew. For many of us is was lost somewhere along the way, along with the patience to cultivate and appreciate it.

Many of us were raised with a limiting 'if – then' formula for happiness. We believe that 'if' we get what we want, 'then' and only then can we be happy. Durable happiness remains illusive when built upon this distorted premise. Using this restricted mantra we have lost the art of anticipation—the enjoyment of looking forward to something whether or not we get what we want in the form we expect it.

In order to move at the hyper–speed demanded by today's accelerated world, we have merged the two joys of 'wanting' something and 'getting' something. By blurring these two experiences in our lives we deprive our children, as well as ourselves, of the simple pleasure of 'looking–forward–to' as a special life skill.

Today the adherence to the 'squeaky wheel gets the grease' theory has sadly become an accepted tenant of life and still is perceived as a prerequisite for success. Both personally and professionally it has resulted in us feeling justified in acts of road rage, intolerance, and violations of our integrity without regret in order to get what we want when we want it. It fertilizes the belief that "if you can't beat 'em, you have to join 'em'" regardless of the price.

THE 'NOW–ALWAYS' FORMULA FOR HAPPINESS

Not having this sense of entitlement and encumbered by the expectation for immediate gratification, preceding generations were perhaps more adept at enjoying present moment living. Patience was a part of how daily life was managed. People expected to work hard toward a delayed goal and learned to appreciate simple pleasures. Practicing patience brought with it the side benefit of noticing the extraordinary in the ordinary and an awareness of the miracles held in each moment. Faced with time pressures and endless stress, it is challenging today to separate and enjoy the two experiences of both wanting and having.

In spite of being a part of a culture too easily annoyed and too often depressed, in our hearts we still long for that same child–like zest for life but haven't quite made the connection between our means affecting the end. Caught in the illusion that what we have is more important than becoming fully who we are, our faith and enthusiasm has become misshapen, seemingly inaccessible, and smothered by ought–o–matics. We let the 'shoulds,' 'have tos' and 'musts' drive our lives.

Think about it! Barely over one hundred years ago it was considered a profound feat to deliver a piece of mail in weeks across the country by pony express. My dad was amazed by the innovation of airmail delivery in less than a week and in awe of the first trip to the moon. Today we now react with frustration when our computer is slow to boot up. We become irritated if there is a momentary delay in sending an e–mail around the world and back through cyber–space in merely a few seconds without moving from our desk.

We focus on what we want, and we want it now! Hmmmmm, what's wrong with this picture?

There is no doubt that life moves faster and faster, but this does not necessitate that we feel victimized. Too often, though, we view life as a battle. Fighting life as it is, and demanding that it be what we think it should be is what drains us. It is not our accelerated pace, but our distorted expectations that create the pressures and disappointments that leave us feeling overwhelmed. We have the opportunity to learn that the circumstances of life are not what matter most. It is the grace with which we handle them. Happiness is not conditional. It is always ours in each moment if we choose to see it. Finally understanding this shifts our direction to keep our eyes focused on the road toward genuine and lasting happiness with peace of mind knowing the 'now'—'always' formula.

Life is a road under construction—expect delays

Procrastinators are often perfectionists in disguise. They avoid beginning until they are certain that they can do it perfectly with the hope of avoiding mistakes as a learning tool. And, then there are perfectionists. They, too, fear failure rather than embrace it as a necessary part of learning life's lessons. Life is always under construction and seldom goes exactly the way we expect. As the saying goes, "Life is what happens while you're making other plans." Don't fight it, life is always under construction. Life is happier when we plan for the unexpected by expecting delays.

Off road traveling

Recalling my experiences as a teen riding dirt bikes in the desert, it became especially tricky after a rain. In an imperceptible instant you could wander off the main trail. The old off-road trails would disappear and new trails would have to be forged, regardless of how accustomed I was to depending on the old path. Interacting with the unknowns rather than resisting them always gave me power and intuition to find my way back to the main trail and find my way home.

Today, in the hurry to get as much done in as little time as possible with perfect results that surpass everyone's expectations, we sometimes wander from our intended route of enjoying now. Even though we may not know how we got detoured from calm to chaos again, there is great significance in the initial recognition that we're 'off course.' This allows us the opportunity to review our map, and yes, even ask for directions! There is magic in the moment we develop the ability to appreciate, accept and find value in what we already have regardless of the circumstances. It actually leads us to having more of what we want. If happiness, calm, and peace of mind are what we want want, with willingness it is guaranteed.

You don't always get what you want,
but you always get what you need

Happiness need not be dependent on getting everything we want according to our own time line, or in the form we expect. Life is full of surprises, and often the surprises are far better than what we ever could have imagined. Lasting joy comes when we learn to focus on what's working, expect miracles, appreciate each and every moment to its fullest, and to recognize the gifts it offers beyond the gifts we expect. It's always wonderful to get what we want, but the experience of longing for something often makes having it much sweeter. After a lengthy anticipation, our appreciation for what we do have becomes more sincere.

We experience lasting happiness when we realize that feeling connected and being here now represent genuine success. They are the greatest assets life has to offer. Peace is ours when we recognize that the most important things in life aren't things, and that love is a choice that is accessible and renewable every moment.

Have you ever run out of gas or had your engine die in the middle of an intersection? You hop out and try to push the car out of harms way, but have less control and a terrible time maneuvering the car from the outside with no internal power and no one at the wheel. So it is with life.

Live your priorities by putting first things first

Prioritizing our values and strengthening our self–confidence from the inside–out offer the clarity we need to direct our vehicle. Our power returns when we risk living what we believe. By having our words and actions match and by making our moment–by–moment decisions based upon this clarity of purpose is what balances the demands of others with our own values and priorities. When we follow our wisdom as our compass and adjust our course to travel the highway of happiness, we love what we have, and therefore have more of what we want.

There is peace in knowing that we are always in the right place at the right time to learn what we are to learn. By participating in life fully and by willingly being all we can be, we participate with life to develop our ability to recognize the joy we would have otherwise let pass us by unnoticed.

Drive yourself happy from the inside out

It's time to climb back behind the wheel of our life and experience it from the inside–out. It is time to resign as a victim of life by accepting the delays and disappointments as well as the wonders and accomplishments. All are vital and valuable parts of our journey. There is no 'there' there. Now is all we really have. Life is right here right now. Happiness is not out on the horizon, but right here, right now, in our heart.

CHAPTER NINE

FUEL
Fill up first.
Always start one more time than you stop.
Small and certain steps motivated by love
and acknowledgments are far greater
fuel for success than speed.

FULL–SERVICE STATIONS ARE A PHENOMENON OF THE PAST. Some of us grew very accustomed to having someone else fill up our tank enabling us to get from one place to another. Now we must fill our own tank. Self–Serve fueling requires our active participation. So does life. Still, we resist and procrastinate.

RUNNING ON EMPTY

Have you ever been in a hurry to get somewhere, then realize that your tank is registering 'empty'? We ignore it as long as possible. If we wait until we are especially pressured, we don't have time to stop. The truth is, we won't get where we want to go if we don't take the time to refuel.

When driving on the sludge and dirt that accumulates at the bottom of the tank, the ride is often rough and our gas mileage inefficient. Eventually stopping is forced upon us. We cannot give from an empty cup, and likewise, we cannot drive on an empty tank.

TURTLE CROSSING

Deciphering inspirational meaning in car metaphors and creating new interpretations for old road signs has become a game for me. A friend, aware of my passion for road signs, sent me a photograph she took on a trip to Hawaii. It was a road sign that read: TURTLE CROSSING.

Although it has been far too long since I last adventured to Hawaii, my memories are vivid. Ideal life there moves at a slower pace and is a vital part of the Hawaiian culture. The people who live there seem to have an awareness and appreciation for the stunning beauty that surrounds them. Years ago I remember, even on the busier freeways, motorists would pull to the side of the road to observe the sunset. They then would resume their journey when the last coral and orange hint of the brilliance of the sun had finished melting into the horizon.

Recalling fondly my high school family vacation in the islands I found it delightful to be reminded with photographic evidence of the cultural present moment priority reflected by a TURTLE CROSSING sign. How wonderful that there is somewhere in the world where people are still willing to slow down, even for turtles. The time spent insuring their safe crossing might seem to some as time wasted, however, there is something valuable for us to consider in this Hawaiian perspective and an important lesson for us to learn from the humble turtles of the world.

A FEW GRAY HARES

Turtles may seem like unlikely teachers, yet the story of the tortoise and the hare is one of my favorite childhood tales. Moving fast has become an expected ingredient of success these days. The value of this fable's message became particularly meaningful for me after a trip to speak for a Fortune 500 corporation on the east coast. I was there to speak about stress management and 'not sweating the small stuff.' Waiting for my time to present, I couldn't help but notice that the person hosting the day was agitated and unraveling at the seams because the agenda as outlined to the minute was running a few minutes behind schedule.

I appreciated his concern for the inconvenience to me because of the time delay, however, I was there to talk about the advantages of present moment living. They had hired me to remind them not to diffuse their energy treating 'small stuff' like 'big stuff.' I assured my host that it was not in my job description to stress over the unexpected delay, and that it was helpful for me to just listen to the remainder of their discussion as a form of preparation for my speech.

I remained calm as the corporate leaders reviewed the statistics that summarized their incredible performance for the past year. A committee chairperson was reporting with surprisingly minimal enthusiasm that the division had met and exceeded their last year's quota by 64%. As I took in the information my internal response was that this was a remarkable accomplishment and certainly warranted accolades. Yet, no pause for acknowledgement was made at this point. I remained hopeful.

As I feared, they moved beyond this fact immediately. Often it is the case in the corporate world that standard protocol dictates even greater expectations for increased efficiency from the 'team' regardless of how high the level of their past performance. The constant 'raising of the bar' is intended to be motivational, but is draining instead. Approval feels very empty and unfulfilling. Lack of acknowledgement leaves us feeling unappreciated and sets the precedent that no matter how hard we work; it will never be hard enough.

Promoted to our level of incompetence

At moments like these we hear reverberations of old and all too often played parental messages that focus on our shortcomings. Although the message is usually delivered with good intention, its impact is more often detrimental and depletes our enthusiasm. Pushed beyond the point of unrealistic expectations where incremental accomplishments are devalued consistently usually results in burnout. To compete, we allow ourselves to be promoted to our level of incompetence. In the corporate world of down–sizing and lay–offs we feel we will eventually be seen as dispensable, replaceable, and no longer an asset.

Their 'pep talk' continued to unfold. The 'team' was

directed by management to project what would be next year's quota. Of course management expected it to exceed last year's performance. Without hesitation or a moment to genuflect in gratitude at the results of this year's hard work, their momentum was coaxed forward beyond the present moment victory by the demands of the future prospectus.

'Busy–holic' burn–out

In such a shortsighted paradigm, success is measured only by outer benchmarks and percentages. It is driven only by relentless forward motion if not initially detoured by resistance and procrastination. I hoped these 'busy–holics' could see the greater power of love, respect, and appreciation as powerful motivations for true success and durable happiness. Fear fueled their sense of urgency and detoured them from seeing that prioritizing the present moment guarantees greater clarity, creativity and constructive growth.

Their faces indicated that their 'engines' were already running on fumes. Pressured by the evidence that they could produce and perform at 64% above last year's 100% projection, they agreed to the challenge to have next year's quota exceed the existing 64% by yet at least another 100%. Racing ahead left no room to celebrate now. When faster is regarded as better, this seems the only logical option—to press forward past the moment, upping the ante every step. Pressure builds to the point that we fail to take authentic action and we ultimately come to believe that we have a choice.

Self–serve success by taking certain small steps

As humans, our greatest natural motivator for loyal, continued and durable success is love. Knowing we belong and that we are appreciated for our contribution feeds our heart and fuels our soul. It gives our life meaning and our heart a sense of purpose. Mistakes are more likely to expediently self–correct when they are expected and honored as a courageous part of attaining success. Ask Henry Ford, Alexander Graham Bell, Jonas Salk, Thomas Edison, or any child falling down a few times in the process of learning to walk. One step at a time our success is honed using mistakes as feedback for further improvement, and unconditional love to nurture our self–confidence.

SUCCESS SELF–SABOTAGE

I am not saying that our lives should be aimless, random, and without goals. Setting high standards and aiming for intentional goals is a very important initial step in taking authentic action. However, setting horrendous goals without acknowledgment and appreciation for incremental steps of applied effort toward greater success at some point only forces us to stress more, produce less, and finally give up. We become disillusioned that we have failed, and are less likely to try again.

Not only at work, but in our personal lives as well we self–generate too much pressure. We multi–task and create the illusion that we're on the road to success when instead we have used unrealistic expectations to set ourselves up for self–sabotage and certain failure—we make our steps too big. How many of us have given ourselves the two weeks before a high school reunion to loose ten pounds? Or, we decide that we are going to set up an exercise program requiring a visit to the gym every day.

It is true that we benefit by stretching beyond our comfort zone and by taking calculated risks, but we must set attainable goals. If we don't chuck them down into incremental and manageable steps we give up before we really begin. we blame others, and hate ourselves for it. In this predictable old scenario at least we have the satisfaction of being right, feeling we weren't capable of or worthy of success anyway!

UNDER–PROMISE AND OVER–DELIVER

Although crossing the finish line is an important ingredient of success, without the courage to start over–and–over, our dreams will never become a reality. So often we detour our energy worrying about what needs to be done in the future rather than just doing it piece–by–piece now. We focus on the overwhelming whole, rather than applying our energy to what needs to be done little–by–little right now. We must break the habit of over–promising and under–delivering, and instead practice under–promising to experience the success of over–delivering. In doing so we will reach our intended goals with far less stress. We can only take the steps of the journey one at a time and will get further with the same number of steps by insuring even the small ones will be successful ones.

Success is starting one more time than you stop

If we begin enough times, focusing on excellence rather than perfection and noticing what is working rather than being critical of what is not, we are certain to get there eventually, and with far greater spirit and self–esteem than when we started. Emphasize success step–by–step, and like the tortoise you will eventually get there with greater grace, efficiency, and integrity. Success is starting one more time than we stop. The confidence we gain will eventually lead us to greater challenges and bigger successes.

CHAPTER TEN

END
The journey is NOW.
Every end is just a new beginning.
Make living your life
more than just making a living.
Realize love is the answer
to every question.

ALTHOUGH MY DAD TAUGHT ME ALMOST EVERYTHING I KNOW about life through his love for cars, it was my mom who provided me with my most essential message for happier living by being with her through her final journey.

A RIGHT WAY, WRONG WAY, AND LYDIA'S WAY

My mom was an amazing businesswoman. She was driven, and throughout her entire life she had measured her worth by her accomplishments. She was beautiful, powerful, generous, and one of the most organized women I have ever known. She was an independent woman before her time, and would often remind us, "There's a right way, a wrong way, and Lydia's way."

She was a working mom when most weren't. My grandmother lived with us to make it possible for my mom and dad to invest whatever hours necessary to run their own business. They were raised by the Great Depression code–of–lack and had a survival work ethic. Wanting the material comforts for us that they never knew motivated them to push their limits. Providing us with 'things' helped calm their feelings of guilt and became their form of compensation for their absence.

Without a doubt, I knew my parents loved me, but still I missed their emotional and physical availability. To express this directly, however, would be misinterpreted as ingratitude for their sacrifices and efforts. Instead, I maintained a silent longing for their undivided attention, and a feeling of sadness for our mutual loss.

Life goes on

We all adapted and life went on. We settled for time together here and there. Although my sister and I, with my parents, would enjoy weekend get–away time in the desert riding go–carts and motorcycles, much of our family time was overshadowed with my parent's discussions about work. When they weren't discussing business they were just flat out exhausted. The pressures of their life left them with little emotional resilience. Even with the best of intentions their actions didn't always follow their words, and promises to us were often broken because business demands regularly took priority.

My mom was dedicated. She worked with greater stamina than any twelve men put together. She was the master at management, juggling the books, hand–posting ledgers, and always magically had whatever you needed in a file box somewhere. Considering how labor intensive her efforts were prior to the advent of computers, her endurance was especially amazing. The message I got was that work was more important.

To cope with the pressures of her 'workaholism,' the accumulative impact of her stress, and her smoking habit since she was barely a teen, my mom maintained her composure with alcohol, or so she thought. Her abuses often made her inaccessible even when her tired body was sitting right before me. Her expectations of herself were unrealistic. Feeling the momentum and responsibility of the business they had started, it was hard for her to slow down. My mom truly was a model of strength with a huge heart of good intentions. Even though her body wore out, it was her heart that finally took her life.

The end of the road

Eighteen months after my dad passed away my mom had her final heart attack. I will be forever grateful to my sister, Debbie. It was because of her nursing expertise that we were able to bring my mom home from the hospital to spend what was to be the last two weeks of her life.

Each moment of these last few days were an amazing paradox of highly accelerated time that seemed to move in slow motion. My mom shared this time with her grandkids, celebrated her last Mother's Day with us, told jokes, fed her dogs snacks they shouldn't eat, and cleaned up a lifetime of unfinished personal business knowing her time was limited. It truly was the most profound two weeks of my life, and I am sure the most remarkable two weeks of hers. During this brief time my mom dissolved and let go of years and years of worry. Her final gift to me was our mutual discovery of the power of the present moment and the importance of now.

AM I COMING OR GOING

"Rhondie, am I coming or going?" she asked in one particular quiet moment in the wee hours of the morning when it was my turn to sit by her bedside in case she needed anything. "That's up to you mom," I responded. "If you feel ready, we are all right here. What's holding you here?" I asked.

"I don't have my taxes filed yet, but what else is new?" she joked. Then after a long pause she shared her more genuine concern. "I told Dana I would come to her high school graduation next month." This clearly was her priority and it was one promise she wanted to keep.

"Don't worry about the taxes, mom. We'll take care of that," I assured her.

"Forget Uncle Sam," she said, "but make sure that Dana knows I'll be at her graduation with or without my body," she declared in her determined way. We just sat there holding hands, and the stillness of the early morning was accentuated by our silence as dark gradually turned to light.

THE PAST DOESN'T MATTER

It seems odd that with all of my training in counseling and

psychology it was me, not my mom, who felt compelled to rehash the past. Feeling a sense of urgency, I believed I must understand in order to make amends. With little breath to spare, she insisted on telling me, "The best way to interrupt a miracle is to insist on understanding before forgiving. Life's too short for that. It's all behind us now" I had never heard such wisdom and sharp clarity from her until NOW.

In response to my attempts during those final days to discuss the past, she would say, "Although I regret the past wasn't different, NOW is all we have, and I don't know how much NOW I have left. Let's not waste it. Be here and present with me right NOW." And so I would, knowing the past didn't really matter anymore, and probably never did.

The future doesn't matter either

During those final two weeks there were times when I would express my sadness to my mom that she would not be able to attend my youngest daughter's graduation, or their weddings, or the birth of her great–grandkids, or just be there when I needed her comforting ear. "I'm sorry I won't be there, too," she would say, "at least not with my body." And, then with a humorous twinkle she added, "But, you can't get rid of me that easily."

With unusual insight and sometimes startling humor she would guide me back to the present moment. She would remind me, "NOW is all I have, so don't waste my NOW asking me to be concerned about the past or the future. Be here present with me right NOW." And so I would, knowing that the future didn't really matter, either.

NOW matters, NOW is where happiness is

In these final moments my mom was teaching me the lessons of a lifetime that somehow made up for all the time I perceived as lost. What we learned together is that all that really matters is the quality of NOW. Life is just one moment after another, one NOW after another. How will we spend them? When we choose to sit in the driver's seat of life fully in the NOW, happiness is ours in that instant, every instant.

Death and birth are monumental moments in our lives. They are remarkably similar in their process. Both involve a transition. Both call forth the opportunity to be who we really are. Both invite great courage, deep faith, and the opportunity to dance with our fears. They bring into play an odd sense of humor, as well as an opportunity for forgiving, and for receiving optimum love and acceptance.

I saw my mom travel several times to the threshold of her passing, and then retreat back to spend a few more days or hours with us. "This time was only a dress rehearsal," she would joke.

With each rally, she traveled ahead again knowing she was approaching her final REST AREA. We encircled her as she declared, "I'm just so tired." I asked if she wanted to rest, and she nodded in affirmation. We leaned her back in her bed, and with her head on my shoulder and my arm around her I had the honor of having her last moment of NOW be spent in my arms. I will never forget those two weeks of one present moment after another.

The present is the gift

This final present moment was the present, the gift. It gave me the assurance that any of the hurts, misunderstandings, or mistakes of the past—hers or mine—were dissolved by pure and unconditional love. We now were free of a lot of baggage. The past and future were moot. We could finally travel light-hearted.

Forgiveness allows us to return to the present moment and sets us free. It's a moment–by–moment choice.

During her conscious dying process, my mom never wished once that she had spent more time at the office. The signifi-cance of her accomplishments were transformed and place in perspective by what seemed genuinely more important. If she had any regrets to heal, it was that she had not prioritized her time along the way with the ones she loved and who loved her in return. She waited until the last moments to awaken to the present moment as her most precious resource. But, now she was awake.

My mother taught me in those conscious moments that NOW can heal all the missed opportunities in an instant. What she held as so important throughout her life, she discovered really wasn't, and what is most important became a profoundly precious priority. Though short when counted in seconds, the wisdom shared in those final days of her life reflected what her life was really all about. Her love was shown as timeless, lasting, and unforgettable.

Living as fully and consciously as we can in the present moment will fuel us with gratitude, the energy for our soul's journey. Living in the present moment we will find assurance that our journey will be purposeful and powerful, and both the journey and the end of the road will bring us happiness regardless of our circumstances.

PART TWO

Signs of Happiness

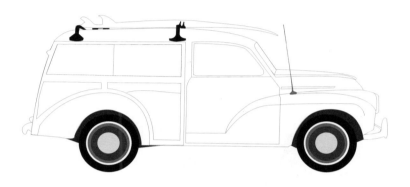

CHAPTER ELEVEN

ADOPT - A - HIGHWAY

ADOPT–A–HIGHWAY

*It is usually not our life
that is 'off course.'
It is the way we think
about our life
that is 'off course.'
Adopt a more positive
vantage point.*

WITH LIFE MOVING SO FAST we've allowed our vision to become distorted. We are short sighted, over–analytical, and have lost touch with it being possible to ADOPT–A–HIGH-WAY of viewing life. We remain determined, instead, to be right rather than happy.

Our 'motor mind' of counter–productive thoughts travels in circles making no progress. Driving in circles wastes gas and wears a deeper rut in our pessimistic perspective. Wanting to have our way, we focus on all that's not working and gather only the evidence that supports our position. We react to both big challenges and small inconveniences as if they were major crises. Like traveling the wrong way on a one–way street, our creativity and compassion disappear into a sea of mental constipation. Life would be so much easier if everyone else would realize they are going the wrong way! From this view-point small things like our partner's dirty socks left on the floor push us over the edge.

When we adopt a fresh viewpoint, like that of a puppy, there need not be problems, only opportunities. When we shift gears, we focus on what's working and experience life from a different perspective. The circumstances may remain the same, but we find freedom in interpreting them differently. Our problems to us become like a dirty pair of socks to a puppy. I haven't met a puppy yet that found a dirty pair of socks annoying. Socks are just socks!

Through the innocence of a puppy's eyes, without judgment or frustration to cloud their perspective, socks are seen as a toy left out for their benefit. Rather than an irritation, the socks become an adventure of unique aromas, something to bury, or enough of an excuse to play and be lighthearted.

When we ADOPT–A–HIGHWAY and make the necessary attitude adjustment in our perception, we realize that there is a different way of viewing life that doesn't make it any harder than it needs to be. Expecting the best rather than focusing on all that could go wrong allows us to more often see through the eyes of innocence, compassion, creativity and caring. Greater happiness follows naturally and with far less effort.

Whenever we pass an ADOPT–A–HIGHWAY road sign, let it be a gentle reminder to clean up the negative thoughts that litter our mind and adopt a happier way of exploring the highway of life.

We're OFF COURSE when:
- We see ourselves as victims of life and blame our parents, our friends, our job, or the circumstances that surround us as the cause of our detours 'off course.' We accuse everyone and everything else as being the reason our lives are not going as we think they should.
- We go along for the ride without taking responsibility for driving, and complain about it rather than participate in life's design.
- We often can't see 'the forest for the trees' and get pulled 'off course' by our negative thinking that takes us on a collision course with fatigue, failure, and frustration.

We're ON COURSE when:

- We learn to adopt a 'big picture' vantage point. Recognizing the power of our thoughts, we take active steps to recognize and clean up our catastrophe thinking. Instead of the old adage of "I'll believe it when I see it," we shift our perception to see the benefit in knowing that "we'll see it when we believe it."

- We focus on what is working, rather than on what is not, knowing that the quality of our thoughts is what creates the quality of our journey. Although weeding out old thoughts may be tedious at times, it is not impossible, and well worth the effort.

It's easier to act your way into a new way of thinking than to think your way into a new way of acting.

—Millard Fuller
founder of Habitat for Humanity

Travel Tips:

- Spend a few days writing down all of the negative thoughts you notice motoring through your mind. Observe them rather than judge them. Becoming conscious of them in a kind way is the first step in slowing down your run–away thoughts. Your gears shift more easily with self–acceptance and willingness.

- Make a list of positive thoughts that can balance or replace the negative thought patterns, and then apply them consciously. Take the wheel. You drive them rather than let them drive you crazy.

- Notice the times, places, people, and situations in which you feel like a victim. Practice seeing them differently or avoid those settings.

- Pay greater attention to when you are playing The Blame Game and determine if you are ANYBODY. Look for ways that you can take greater responsibility for putting yourself back in the driver's seat of your life.

The Blame Game

Once upon a time, there were four people.
Their names were
EVERYBODY,
SOMEBODY,
NOBODY and
ANYBODY.

Whenever there was an important job to be done,
EVERYBODY was sure that
SOMEBODY would do it.
ANYBODY could have done it, but
NOBODY did it.

When NOBODY did it,
EVERYBODY got angry because it was
EVERYBODY'S job.
EVERYBODY thought that
SOMEBODY would do it, but
NOBODY realized that
NOBODY would do it.

So, consequently,
EVERYBODY blamed
SOMEBODY when
NOBODY did what
ANYBODY could have done in the first place.

—Author unknown (Could be ANYBODY)

CHAPTER TWELVE

CROSS TRAFFIC AHEAD:
Be compassionate with irritable people
especially if that irritable person is you.
When fearful we either run or fight.
Be willing to face life, and open
to learn its lessons.

IT SEEMS SOMETIMES LIKE THE ENTIRE WORLD IS IRRITABLE, ill–tempered, and cross, including us. When we encounter CROSS TRAFFIC AHEAD we mistake what appears as an obstacle to be the cause of all our problems and a reason for defensiveness and retaliation. We often see life and the people in it as one continuing annoyance rather than recognizing the part we play. We often create life as a drama by our over–reactions and misinterpretations. Fueled by our fatigue we lose our compassion and become defensive causing our happiness to disappear. We get stuck in believing that someone or something outside of us must change before our perception can become more positive and our experience can improve. Unknowingly, we become our own roadblock to joy.

We attempt to deal with roadblocks in three different ways:
   1. We pull off the road. Some of us react by being over–sensitive. We disengage and personalize the bad moods of others, feel victimized, and avoid conflict, certain there will be no satisfactory resolution. We run from situations afraid we will make a mistake and expecting to be hurt. In our attempts to run from life, we are tormented by it. We fear change and blame other's for our problems.
   2. We drive into oncoming traffic. Others engage in conflict as a competitive battle of one upmanship where one must win and one must lose, certain that we are right. We use our judgments and criticisms as an illusion of knowing what is

best. We squander energy and misuse our time by resisting. We are self–absorbed, selfish and committed to be the victor with little consideration for the impact of our words and actions on another. Worst of all we let these encounters or avoidances ruin our day, week, month—or even our life. In our efforts to control life, it controls us.

3. We go with the flow of traffic. Some are ready to embrace life and travel with it, rather than run or resist. We embrace mistakes and feedback for growth. We are willing to learn life's lessons sooner rather than later. We have faith that the lessons of life are loving and beneficial, trust that they can be simple rather than hard, and surrender to love rather than resisting it. We give up the struggle and focus on the wonders of life. We see blessings regardless of challenging circumstances.

Being ready to run or ready to fight are both driven by fear. Holding resentments and avoiding a relationship with ourselves is a waste of life and only keeps us a prisoner in our false perceptions. Forgiveness and being willing to face life's unknowns with wonder and grace are the keys to finding flow in the traffic of life. When we forgive others and ourselves more quickly for our lapses of consciousness and thoughtless insensitivities, willing to apply what we have learned to expand loving possibilities in our life, it truly becomes a joy ride.

Whenever we see the road sign CROSS TRAFFIC AHEAD, let it be a subtle reminder that we need not be a victim or a victor, but can become an active partner with life. With a willing and open heart life becomes a joy ride rather than a destruction derby.

We're OFF COURSE when:

- We defend every verbal assault and resolve every conflict, fighting until we have successfully become the victor regardless of who we hurt in the process.
- We let the bad mood of another easily stick on us, and we blame them for ruining our day. We react defensively and lose our ability to respond with compassion.
- We are irritable and reactive usually because we are fearful. We interrupt to defend our position, rather than listen with true interest in seeing from the perspective of another.
- We run, take no action or react inappropriately.

We're ON COURSE when:

- We acknowledge bad moods, and let them pass like the weather without giving them the power to ruin our day.
- We wear a Teflon raincoat, and let the petty comments, insensitive gestures, unintentional mistakes and bad moods of others, slide off without carrying any residue resentment.
- We respond to conflict with a strong, but calm demeanor and with an intention to find resolution.
- We stand as far away from someone as necessary to remain loving. Sometimes the most loving thing you can do for yourself and another is to give them some time alone.
- We forgive at the earliest possible opportunity, and apply what we learn from our transgressions.
- We remain committed and willing to grow and courageously take authentic action in that direction.

Travel Tips:

- When you find yourself over–reacting to someone, or any given situation, look for what is 'off course' in your life that makes you willing to hand over your personal power to another. What irritates you about another is often a reflection of what upsets you about yourself, or a lesson waiting to be learned. If you have a 'blow out' because someone is late, ask yourself if you are always on time and keep your agreements. Use the insensitivity and reactivity of another as the opportunity to clean up your own reactivity. Practice expanding your ability to respond with compassion knowing that people who are inconsiderate are usually afraid about something.

- When you are trapped in a bad mood remember it is like pollution. Don't spread your smog around. Acknowledge your mood without judging it, and know you may not always understand why it has affected you. Do not resist it, empower it or attach to it by getting enraptured by it's drama. Release it as soon as possible, letting it pass on through. Left alone, like the weather, moods will pass.

CHAPTER THIRTEEN

KEEP CLEAR
Make clarity a priority.
Be clear and centered within yourself.
People will only love and respect you
to the degree to which
you love and respect yourself.

WHAT DO WE WANT? What does genuine happiness mean to us? Focused on taking care of all of the people and things in our busy lives, we become clearer on their expectations than on what is important and meaningful to us.

Often, we fail to KEEP CLEAR our own core values and lose connection with what is of greatest value to us. There seems to be a real epidemic of apathy and unworthiness that detours us from honoring ourselves, finding a sense of purpose, and living our life with clarity and enthusiasm. We forget how to turn down the buzz of our stressful world in order to access our inner wisdom. We are conditioned to look outside of ourselves for the answers, rather than 'drive–in' to find our direction and peace of mind.

We confuse being self–centered—clear and centered within ourselves, with being selfish—focused on satisfying our needs and wants at the expense of another. When we love and honor others more than we love and honor ourselves, the delight of giving eventually turns to resentment. Giving from a place of resentment is like trying to drive a car when the fuel tank is empty. It just doesn't work. What you give is no longer a gift and generates guilt. It becomes an obstacle course of anger, fatigue, and misunderstanding. The truth is that we cannot nurture the Spirit of another until we can nurture our own.

Our clarity is actually one of the most important gifts we can give those we love. When we maintain our own balance, we have the energy to share who we really are authentically.

We offer a true gift when we expect nothing in return and find our gift in the giving.

When we see the KEEP CLEAR road sign, let it be a reminder to treat ourselves with love and respect as the pre-requisite to offering a genuine gift of time and love to another. When we nurture our self–confidence and expand our inner wisdom we are better able to serve others by sharing the radiance of our happiness.

We're OFF COURSE when:
- We find ourselves frazzled and short–tempered, going a hundred different directions, doing too many things at once, with only the illusion of getting anything done.
- Our performance becomes scattered and inefficient.
- We often take our frustrations out on the ones we love the most, expecting them to understand no matter how badly we treat them.
- The first thing we eliminate from our routine when we're in a time crunch is the quiet time or activities that renew our Spirit most.
- We push ourselves by 'shoulds,' 'have tos' and 'musts.' We ignore the signals offered by our body that we are 'running on fumes.' We ignore our intuition saying it's time to re–prioritize for greater calm and happiness.
- Often we get sick, have an accident, or something even worse as a dramatic way of remembering value of being still and the importance of maintaining balance in our life.
- We start and end our day on the news report of hate, mayhem and disaster and thrive on drama. We wonder why we're so anxious and apathetic. We become numb to the assaults, and often depend on alcohol, drugs, or TV as the excess necessary to cover our dissatisfaction and sadness.
- We respond to help with resistance, say things we don't really mean, answer questions with biting comments, and often don't realize the damage we are causing to our relationships.

We're ON COURSE when:

- We understand that enjoying our own company and learning to be still are essential keys to happiness. We make personal growth a priority, and make quiet, meditation and reflection time a non–negotiable part of our day, like brushing our teeth.
- We monitor our environment, being sure to balance all of the negative input that surrounds us with positive people, inspirational reading, and time doing the things we love. When we risk putting first things first, we discover that we actually have more time, greater productivity, stronger relationships, and a more meaningful and conscious life.
- We surround ourselves with equally committed people and acknowledge our loved ones for their support and friendship.
- We are satisfied with excellence, rather than not accepting ourselves unless we are perfect.

Travel Tips:

- Create a list of your priorities—mentally, physically, spiritually and emotionally. Write down one small thing you can accomplish in the next week in each of these areas that will nurture you and make you feel that your life has had meaning.
- Pick up your calendar or palm pilot right now and schedule meetings with yourself, as well as time for significant relationships. Dare to experiment with truly putting first things first. Do not be tempted to carve from your time with yourself those extra minutes to squeeze one more thing into your already over booked calendar. Leave space for the unexpected to happen. Plot the rest of your schedule around your 'priority appointments' with yourself.
- STOP before something like cancer or a heart attack stops you. Get clear on what is most important to you. Spend five minutes writing the elegy to be read at your memorial service that reflects what people will learn by how you lived your life.

Remember that the most important things in life are not things—not your money, your car, your job or your house. They are your relationships. Use authentic and mutual relationships as fuel for your journey, knowing that when we put first things first—like the people we love—we are more certain to enjoy both the journey and the destination, never feeling alone.

CHAPTER FOURTEEN

DO NOT PASS

DO NOT PASS
*Experience the freedom of neutral
and trust that you are always
in the right place at the right time
regardless of how it appears.*

DO NOT PASS UP CALM AND QUIET MOMENTS. What we need most is the stillness to hear our inner wisdom. Often unconsciously we fuel our 'motor mind.' We justify worry as a form of planning. This keeps our priorities out of order and distracts us from living life consciously.

When we need to find time to meet one more deadline in our busy day, we are too quick to forfeit the introspective time that renews us. We see giving up time with ourselves as the easiest solution to juggle the demands of our over–scheduling woes. We manage to squeeze in the time to brush our teeth and shower so we look good from the outside, but soon feel empty inside because we have neglected ourselves from the inside out.

We must prioritize and honor our need for time alone as a necessary opportunity to review what we really want, and then move steadfastly in that direction regardless of backward steps from time to time.

When we travel along the highway and see the road sign DO NOT PASS, let it be the reminder not to pass up the opportunity to appreciate what is right before us. Rather than race through life and demean the value of introspective time, remember our peace of mind lies within that stillness inside of us that's accessible by taking time to renew our Spirit. Make more conscious choices about how you spend your time, putting first things first and making renewal time a priority.

We're OFF COURSE when:

- We practice multi–tasking mania, and pride ourselves in doing twelve things at once. We do so with scattered attention rather than focusing on one thing thoughtfully at a time and usually are irritable and unapproachable. Pushed by the expectations of others, we eventually promote ourselves to our level of incompetence. In the process we jeopardize our health and relationships. We feel frazzled that all our efforts have accomplished no more than spinning in place with a trunk full of self–criticism as our only companion.
- We develop a skewed sense of entitlement and intolerance, thinking we deserve to have life the way we want it when we want it. We act as if our needs are more important than any one else's. We lose sight of our inner signals to pace ourselves and always seem to want more than we have. Nothing feels satisfying or good enough.
- Trapped by worry, we are seldom consciously in the present moment. We go through the motions of life numb and without enthusiasm.
- We see life as one problem after another.

We're ON COURSE when:

- We choose to be conscious and present moment oriented. From this place of greater clarity we make wise decisions and pace ourselves in a loving and productive way, enjoying all that we do and appreciating all that we have.
- We develop our ability to see the extraordinary in the ordinary and view problems as opportunities to learn. We realize that when we want what we have, we have what we want.
- We honor others' needs rather than hold our needs as important as anyone else's.
- We recognize that taking a ride on the worry wheel is a waste of our precious energy. We consciously apply gratitude as our antidote for worry.

Travel Tips:

- Find NEUTRAL. Be in that moment of suspended animation that is neither attached to the past or the future. Notice all of the times your thoughts take you to your past, or your worries take you into the future in a non–productive way. Practice lovingly and gently redirecting yourself to the present. Learn to focus on rather than cope with the task before you. Contrary to what we have learned, being focused on one thing at a time fully brings greater success and productivity than doing many things with scattered attention. Enjoy the benefits of quality, not quantity.

- When trapped on the 'wheel of worry,' write each one down and play the 'What if...' game. To get out of the loop, ask yourself what would happen 'if' each worry were to come true. Inquire as many times as needed to determine what really is your bottom line fear. Honestly ask yourself how likely it is to happen and how realistic is your fear. Remember, FEAR is often **F**alse **E**xpectations **A**ppearing **R**eal.

- Ask what the circumstances call you to learn about yourself. Handle what is real with grace and expand your willingness to grow.

- To reverse your worries into blessings, write down three things for which you are grateful. Practice this as your antidote until your worries subside and are replaced with the habit of caring and calm.

My life has been filled with terrible misfortunes, most of which never happened. Life does not consist mainly, or even largely—of facts and happenings. It consists mainly of the storm of thoughts that is forever blowing through one's head.

—Mark Twain

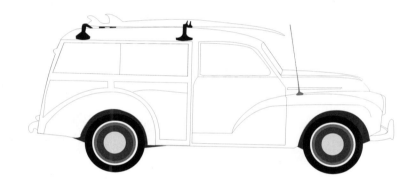

CHAPTER FIFTEEN

DON'T BACK UP

SEVERE
TIRE DAMAGE
MAY OCCUR

DON'T BACK UP, SEVERE TIRE DAMAGE MAY OCCUR

Don't live life in reverse.
Reliving your past with blame
and resentment is self–destructive.
Now is the only moment you really have.
Live it up!

SO MANY OF US ATTEMPT TO NAVIGATE LIFE by trying to drive forward while looking out the back window! Driving backward into the past may puncture our emotional tires. We live now as if it were then with all the fear compounded by time. This causes us to relive our past in a way that guarantees it will become our future. Even though it no longer serves us, it is predictable and familiar, and therefore alluring.

On our trip through life we often carry far too much left over emotional baggage. So much energy is exhausted bemoaning what we cannot change, blaming all the facets of our past for our current problems, and anticipating our future to be a repeat performance. Even if our childhood was filled with disappointments and bad guidance, we need not relive its pain That was then, this is now. We can learn from the past without needing to live there again.

Like it or not, we often learn some of our most valuable lessons of life by maneuvering our challenging times. By visiting the past for clues, rather than to repeat and relive the dysfunctional patterns, we resign from our role of victim. Horrendous hurts from the past need no longer paralyze us when we see the opportunity to heal using the 'the gift of opposites.' By being very clear on what did not work then, we have the structure that will guide us in adjusting our path toward the future now. Implementing the opposite of the shortcomings of the past becomes a healthier now. Making now a more enjoyable place to be offers a comforting purpose for the challenges of the past that allows us to move forward freely and with forgiveness.

DO NOT BACK UP—SEVERE TIRE DAMAGE MAY OCCUR is a sign that carries a powerful message that reminds us to learn from our past and to value the present moment.

We're OFF COURSE when:
- We constantly relive the wounds and assaults of the past. We do not forgive, and make our resentment evident. We are bitter. We let our unresolved issues negatively impacts our current relationships, our job, and our relationship with ourselves.
- We expect the future to be a repeat of the past, and therefore expect the worst possible outcome.
- Unable to forgive others and ourselves we tend to repeat poor judgments and patterns of the past.
- We continue to try the same things over and over while expecting different results.
- We miss out on the wonders that are right before us, distracted by our attachment to the past.

We're ON COURSE when:
- We look to the past for clues about what we can change now and take positive steps to make the present more than a repeat of the past.
- We apply the 'gift of opposites. We recognize that each wound and transgression of our past offers insight about what we can shift in our lives now to generate a happier future.
- We forgive others and ourselves easily, willingly knowing that forgiveness brings freedom and peace of mind. We understand that judgments and grudges hold us hostage.

- We understand that forgiveness does not mean that we condone inappropriate actions or tolerate abuse of any kind. We love and forgive someone with enough space between us to insure we are not treated with disrespect. We speak up when necessary to be heard. When we forgive, we set ourselves free.

Success is the ability to go from one failure to another with no loss of enthusiasm.

—Winston Churchill (1874 - 1965)
British Prime Minister

Travel Tips:
- Make a list of at least five things that your parents or someone of significance in your life did 'wrong' to you as a child.
- Make a list of the ways you allow those transgressions to still limit you currently.

Now, assume that there is a gift or clue for your growth in each transgression. By pinpointing the opposite of what didn't work, then you can start the adventure of redesigning now differently. When you begin to see that the past offers you insights applicable to make a better now, even though it is through opposites, you begin to perceive the gift, returning you to gratitude and peace.

CHAPTER SIXTEEN

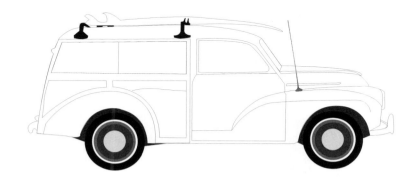

EQUESTRIAN CROSSING

Instead of expecting manure in life,
look for the pony.
What you see is what you get.
Believing is seeing.

OUR RESILIENCE HANDLING THE UNCERTAINTIES OF LIFE is expanded when we know we have a choice in how we view them. However, many of us fight life instead and feel beat up by it. We react as if life is an enemy to be feared, fled, or fought rather than learning to dance with it. Rather than joy, what we experience is exhaustion and 'a–void–dance'—dancing in the void of emptiness. We spend our time shoveling the manure in life, rather than looking for the pony!

The truth is that we do not always have control over the circumstances of our life, but we always have influence over how we view them. We make the mistake of believing that not until the circumstances of life are in order can we change our attitude and become more positive and happy. It is foolish to wait! Life is too short. A step toward happiness is realizing we really do get to choose our attitude.

That's not to say that there won't be challenges and upsets. From time to time there are painful periods that are certain to block our access to joy. Guaranteed! Without acknowledging that we're hurting and facing it in some way, we become blinded by denial. It's when we choose to notice and focus on the things in our life that are working, especially when the circumstances that surround us seem to be overwhelming, that we become able to experience dependable joy. Our greatest happiness comes when we are open to the lessons of life even when life is harsh.

When we come to a horse crossing and notice the EQUESTRIAN sign, let us be reminded to 'look for the pony.' Expect joy even amidst challenging times, and look for it hidden in small and unexpected ways. When we take responsibility for our focus, we will be delighted with the expansion of our happiness. When we fully understand and take responsibility for being at choice for how we see the circumstances of our life, we are back in the driver's seat of life, ready to apply our true power.

We're OFF COURSE when:
- We are so focused on what is not working in our life, that we loose sight of all that is working. Whining becomes habitual. Even if ninety–nine things went right during the day, what we talk about over dinner is the one thing that went wrong.
- We are trapped in catastrophe thinking, and take life way too seriously. We feel that having fun will prevent us from being effective.
- We never give ourselves a break, failing to take time for the things that renew our spirit and give us energy.
- We are attached to drama, blame, and worry, and resist seeing another viewpoint.
- We always have evidence to defend our pessimistic perspective and feel guilty when we feel happy.

We're ON COURSE when:
- We expand our ability to focus on what is working with an understanding that what we focus on we create more of.
- Even when the circumstances are tough or we are faced with a loss or disappointment, we trust that there is ultimately a gift of insight and growth available to us, even if it takes awhile to become evident.
- We recognize that faith is a more dependable companion than logic when we are faced with what appears to be insurmountable odds. Contrary to being taught that 'seeing

is believing,' we now find greater happiness by applying the new perspective with certainty that 'believing is seeing.'

- We know that the need to understand is often what distracts us from the miracle. We trust our intuition more, and allow ourselves to be still often enough to recognize our inner voice and hear its wisdom.
- We assume life is good and look for the innocence in others.
- We become aware of our tendency to be judgmental and defensive. We know that only when we have the ability to lighten up, become less stubborn and resistant, and open our eyes to expand our positive perspective, will we be able to access lasting happiness.
- We trust the process of life.

The greater part of happiness or misery depends on our dispositions, and not on our circumstances.

—Martha Washington

Travel Tips:
- What do you read at first glance in these letters?
  I A M N O W H E R E
- Did you read: I AM NOWHERE
  or I AM NOW HERE?

The ten letters are the same regardless of which way we read them. We can read them as a positive statement or a negative one. No one forces us to see it a particular way. We choose.

CHAPTER SEVENTEEN

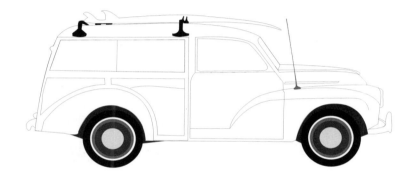

NO OUTLET
We will crash without an outlet.
Enjoy life, learn to play.
We think we don't have time.
The truth is we don't have time not to!
Fill yourself up.

WE LIVE LIFE IN A CONSTANT STATE OF HURRY. There doesn't seem to be time for happiness now. In our perpetual busy–ness we look productive but get surprisingly little done. Our scattered focus is just a way of avoiding ourselves and the issues that are of true importance. Detoured by the illusion of importance caused by our busy–ness, we postpone doing the things that would renew our Spirit and fill us with energy. We regard the things that touch our heart and bring us renewal as a frivolous use of our time. Pushed by 'musts' we see no other option than self–sacrifice. Renewal, relationships, and matters of heart are always put off thinking there will be time later.

'Later' often never comes. Without outlets for our stress and opportunities for self–renewal we eventually come to a grinding halt or crash and burn, hurting the ones we love along the way. Too often we are cut short and left with regrets. It is time to dispel the myth. We are far more productive, efficient, and creative when we live life consciously, face obstacles, have outlets, appreciate our support system, and put first things first. Our task at hand is to enjoy the journey and plan for the future by living life as consciously as we would if we knew we might die tomorrow.

We're OFF COURSE when:
- We allow our limited thinking to assassinate our creativity, rather than think 'outside the box,' enlisting our intuition to find creative solutions.
- We settle for using cheap fuel and look for a quick fix.
- We force ourselves forward, ignoring all of the signals that our fuel is low and our gas gauge is reading EMPTY.
- We tax our engine until it blows up as a forced way of slowing down.
- We are easily irritated, totally depleted of energy and often non–productive despite long hours of work.
- We think having fun is a waste of time.

We're ON COURSE when:
- We fully recognize that enjoying an OUTLET or diversion can renew our creativity, allowing us to return to our work with more energy and creativity.
- The line between work and play becomes fuzzier, and we incorporate joy and playfulness into the work that we do regularly, trusting it will improve our performance. We see personal joy as an asset and honor it as an essential ingredient of success.
- We see our work as our choice, rather than believing we are a victim of our employment, co–workers, or boss.
- We get more done in less time, and find satisfaction in our accomplishments, less frazzled by minor detours.
- We show up alive, fully who we are, and invested in life, rather than full of resistance.
- We greet each morning with our prayer being, "Good morning, God," rather than, "Good God, morning!"

Sing as though no one is listening.
Live as though heaven is on earth.
Work like you don't need money.
Love like you've never been hurt.
Dance as if nobody is watching.

—Author Unknown

Travel Tips:
- List twenty things you love to do.
- Note the last time you did any of them. In the last week? Month? Year?
- Did you do it alone or with someone?
- Which ones required planning?
- Note which one costs money. How much? More than $20? Less than $20?
- Take out your calendar now and schedule a date with yourself to do at least one of the things that you love, big or small. Guard that date as if it were with a holy person. It is.
- List at least 100 things you would like to do, big or small, before you die and then enjoy being creative in your manifestation process.
- Check in with yourself every month and review your list.

CHAPTER EIGHTEEN

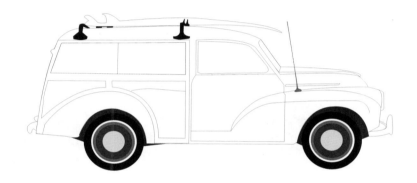

BOAT LAUNCH RAMP
Row, row, row your boat,
Gently down the stream.
Merrily, merrily, merrily, merrily.
Life is but a dream ...
So, go with the flow of traffic.

WE ARE ALL PROBABLY FAMILIAR with this children's nursery rhyme, but never considered Mother Goose might be a guru, until now. Her words are very wise. Whether it was her intention or not, this short song offers an easy to remember formula for being happy. By singing it in rounds, we are reminded that any missed or ignored opportunities for growth will most certainly come around again. This nursery rhyme offers a lighthearted way of keeping us on course.

Row, Row, Row Your Boat invites us to address our own challenges, rather than attempting to control another's problems as a way of avoiding our own issues.

Gently Down the Stream reminds us that life can be simple. When free of our resistance we can more easily find creative solutions and take authentic action. This does not mean we look for the easy way out or avoid challenges, but look for the way that best honors our intuition rather than our 'motor mind.' Life is happiest when we flow with change, rather than resist it.

Merrily, Merrily, Merrily, Merrily points us in the direction of joy. We will find greater balance when we lighten up, laugh often, and discipline ourselves. Fill each day with ample amounts of laughter and inspiration to counter–balance all of the negative input and depressing news.

Life is But a Dream reminds us that our imagination is our only limitation. It is not the circumstances that create our life; it is how we respond to the circumstances that create our life. We will be happier when we adjust our negative thinking, assume responsibility for our direction and dare to dream big, followed by incremental action steps bathed in faith.

Although most of us do not frequently see a sign indicating a BOAT LAUNCH, it is one worth keeping in mind. This sign can be a unique reminder to stay focused on the wonders of life. It suggests we reroute resistance to allow life to be a gentle experience, to love and laugh often, and to embrace that we create our reality by the quality of our thoughts.

We're OFF COURSE when:
- We judge the success of our life by comparing it to the life of another or question the progress of another by our judgments and perception of how life 'should' be.
- We gravitate toward conflict. We somehow see value in the drama, and experience life as a struggle each and every day.
- We are always hyper–vigilant and expect life to be hard. Even when it is not hard, we make it so.
- We resist rather than surrender, and must understand before we move ahead or forgive.

We're ON COURSE when:
- We are fascinated by differences and appreciate alternative perspectives of others without feeling our own is threatened.
- We see the highest and best in others and trust their positive intention.

82

- We teach best by attending to our own challenges with grace. We don't fix or problem solve for another without a request or permission. We honor the learning process of another, even when they choose for it to be more difficult than it needs to be.
- We use our degree of calm and simplicity as a way of determining how far we are off course.
- We learn to trust the flow of life and surrender without feeling like we are giving up.

Travel Tips:
- Reroute resistance. What we resist persists. What if you trust that the outcome is always as it should be, even when it is not apparent or in the form you expected? Practice believing all is as it should be.
- Recognize the shortcomings of others not as an invitation for you to fix them, but as an opportunity for you to observe and fine–tune your own engine.
- When we surrender our need to control, we can go with the flow and recognize the unexpected miracles. Practice letting go, and look for the gift in every situation.
- Life is too serious to take it all seriously. Today, laugh often and for no apparent reason. Better yet, share a laugh with someone.

CHAPTER NINETEEN

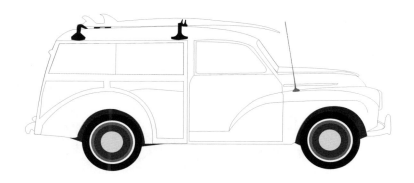

DEAD END

We can't usually control how we die,
but we can decide how we live.
How we live is a choice—
a moment–by–moment choice.
So, choose.

WE LIVE IN A CULTURE THAT STRUGGLES to reverse the aging process. We have been taught that who we are and our degree of worth are determined by the how young we look and condition of our body. We cling to our youth. We spend millions of dollars trying to control the aging process, resisting rather than appreciating our maturity. Trapped by our fear, we focus on what we are losing rather than embracing the opportunities we gain to be eccentric, demonstrative and unique.

Like it or not the fact of life remains that sometimes life is hard, not fair, our body wears out, and our memory falters. Bad things sometimes happen to good people, and grief is a part of the process no matter how much money we have. No matter how much you have in your bank account, no one gets out alive! We blame these things as the reasons for our frustration and despair, but what drains us and makes us unhappy is not that these things are true, but that we can't control them. We set in place the condition that life must be manageable for us to be happy.

The good news is that we can be happy amidst change, and are not alone in facing this challenge. We all face the process of aging, we all experience loss, and we all face the challenges of the mysteries and unknowns of life. We can spend the time we have wishing it were different, or search for the ways to make it meaningful. You can make a life, or settle for just making a living. You can stay in denial and live in fear until you die, or just live. You decide.

The DEAD END sign reminds us that every moment counts. We can gain and lose money over and over, but the time we have here is truly a limited commodity. Choose to make the best of it and give the most to it to enjoy durable happiness.

We're OFF COURSE when:
- We use a tremendous amount of energy resisting and complaining about what is, finding ourselves exhausted, defensive and reactive.
- We fight depression and apathy when life does not go as we planned. We are critical and judgmental, easily finding fault with others while overlooking our contribution to insuring conflict. We look back, rather than proactively move forward.
- We effort to control because we are fearful of change and tend to sabotage our personal growth and success by staying firmly attached to our 'comfort zone.' We only see evidence to support our viewpoint. Life is played as a game of 'win–lose.'
- We easily waver in our integrity in order to have what we want.

We're ON COURSE when:
- We take personal responsibility for making our life meaningful, and insist that our words and actions match.
- We dare to take risks, and are always open to adjusting our viewpoints, supporting life as a game of 'win–win.'
- We move confidently, boldly, compassionately, and actively in the direction of our dreams and values. We walk beyond our fears and limiting beliefs to see life as having limitless possibilities.
- We take the time to listen objectively without judgment knowing communication is more than just waiting for our turn to talk. We develop our ability to listen beyond the words being spoken.
- We know when we have reached a DEAD–END. We surrender with grace, willing to receive the lesson sooner than later and with greater grace.

Travel Tips:
- Do you need to forgive anyone? What are you waiting for?
- List at least five ways you currently make life harder than it needs to be.
- What do you plan to do about it? By when?
- What do you want to be remembered for as your greatest accomplishments?
- Write a commencement address. What would you say to students to guide and motivate them in living a happy life?

CHAPTER TWENTY

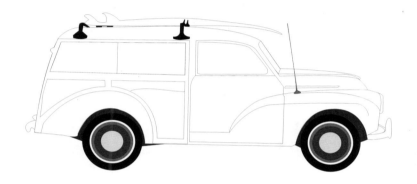

REST AREA

Rest is an indispensable ingredient of success.
Pause for simple things.
Change your heart and your mind when you cannot change your circumstances.

BALANCE BETWEEN WORK AND FAMILY becomes only an illusion when we are driven by the mis–belief that if we just run fast enough and multi–task long enough we will empty our in–basket and check everything off our list.

Happiness comes only when we dare to stop, and rest long enough to rejuvenate and prioritize the things that are truly important in our life. The first priority is to put the first things first, the second is to remember that the most important things in life aren't things.

The REST AREA road sign invites us to remember that we actually become more productive, creative, compassionate and effective when we rest long enough to regain our strength and reconnect with our wisdom. We will benefit by resisting the thought that we don't have time and view rest as an important ingredient of success.

FIVE BALLS

by Brian G. Dyson, President and CEO
Coca–Cola Enterprises
(Georgia Tech Commencement Ceremony, 1991)

"Imagine life as a game in which you are juggling some five balls in the air. You name them WORK, FAMILY, HEALTH, FRIENDS and SPIRIT, and you're keeping all of these in the air. You will soon understand that WORK is a rubber ball. If you drop it will bounce back. But the other four balls—FAMILY, HEALTH, FRIENDS and SPIRIT—are made of glass. If you drop one of these, they will be irrevocably scuffed, marked, nicked, damaged, or even shattered. They will never be the same. You must understand to strive for balance in your life. How?

- Don't underestimate your worth by comparing yourself with others. It is because each of us is different that each of us is special. Don't set your goals by what other people deem important. Only you know what is best for you.
- Don't take for granted the things closest to your heart. Cling to them as your would your life, for without them, life is meaningless.
- Don't let your life slip through your fingers by living in the past or for the future. By living your life one day at a time, you live ALL the days of your life.
- Don't give up when you have something to give. Nothing is really over until the moment you stop trying.
- Don't be afraid to admit that you are less than perfect. It is this fragile thread that binds us together.
- Don't be afraid to encounter risks. It is by taking chances that we learn to be brave.
- Don't shut love out of your life by saying it's impossible to find. The quickest way to receive love is to give; the fastest way to lose love is to hold it too tightly; and the best way to keep love is to give it wings.
- Don't run through life so fast you forget not only where you've been, but also where you are going.
- Don't forget that a person's greatest emotional need is to feel appreciated.
- Don't be afraid to learn. Knowledge is weightless, a treasure you can always carry easily.
- Don't use time or words carelessly. Neither can be retrieved.

- Life is not a race, but a journey to be savored each step of the way.

Yesterday is History, Tomorrow is a Mystery, and Today is a Gift: That's why we call it the Present."

We're OFF COURSE when:
- We live life in a chaotic and agitated state of drama and think it's normal.
- We focus on obscure goals, and move at such a rapid pace that we fail to enjoy the simple things along the way.
- We operate under the illusion that we will be able to complete all of the tasks on our list, and then we will have time to enjoy our life focused on family and friends.
- Often we damage our health and our relationships, setting our accomplishments as the measurement of our worth.
- We believe that if we slow down, we will never find the energy to begin again.
- We see happiness as something to be enjoyed at the end of the road, and often fail to celebrate small victories along the way.

We're ON COURSE when:
- We strive for peace, calm and excellence rather than for perfection.
- We balance work and play, knowing that taking the time to rest energizes us with greater creativity, compassion, and productivity.
- We are spontaneous, imaginative, and easily think 'outside the box.'
- We see that sadness and disappointment offer us a deeper appreciation of happiness. We welcome darkness as a insightful part of the light and know that happiness includes both. We understand that happiness does not

disappear, but encompasses both highs and lows. It frees us to be happy regardless of our circumstances.

- More accepting of the mysteries of life, and needing less to manipulate and control it, we focus on quality rather than quantity.
- We appreciate the miracles available in the present moment and commit to happy living.

Travel Tips:
- Create a REST STOP in your daily routine. Work into your schedule at least ten minutes in the morning and ten minutes in the evening to begin and end your day in a centered and conscious way. Live your commitment, and demonstrate to yourself and everyone else that you are worth being loved and respected.
- Put spontaneity back into your life. Do something unexpected, like swing, skip, whistle, sing in the shower, fly a kite—be playful every chance you get.
- Do a random act of kindness everyday without expecting anything in return.
- Take a nap, have a cup of tea, or treat yourself to a regular REST STOP. Actually schedule time with yourself and mark it on your calendar. Honor the date with yourself as if you had an appointment with a holy person. When people want to schedule with you during your time, tell them you have already booked a very important date that you cannot rearrange. Your heart appreciates being valued, especially by you.

CHAPTER TWENTY–ONE

CURB YOUR WHEELS

PREVENT RUNAWAYS

CURB YOUR WHEELS— PREVENT RUN–AWAYS

First gear—notice negative thoughts.
Second gear—be kind to yourself.
Third gear—pay attention to the highway.
Fourth gear—choose happiness.
Love is neutral. Don't drive in reverse.

LIKE A CAR THAT HAS LOST ITS BRAKES ON A HILL, our thoughts can veer out of control and pick up momentum along the way. They can cause destruction and chaos as a result of their uncharted and haphazard path downward. Until now, we feel obligated to follow every thought. Placing our attention on the drama rather than on the delight of life, what we focus on we create more of. To stabilize your life CURB YOUR WHEELS—PREVENT RUN–AWAY thoughts.

It is time to impose some discipline on our thoughts rather than letting them run wild in control of our well–being. But, for many of us, discipline conjures up a negative meaning with images of punishment and failure rather than positive guidance and welcome direction. It's important to redefine discipline to begin to appreciate its true value.

The word discipline is derived from the word disciple. A disciple is a guide, one who leads the way with unconditional love. Discipline can be a strong and centering force rather than one that motivates by fear. Instead of blame and degrading reprimand, our thoughts need gentle re–direction and loving re–parenting. This allows us to shift gears, taking a new road to greater and more durable happiness.

The CURB YOUR WHEELS—PREVENT RUN–AWAYS road sign greets us with its message on the more slippery slopes of life. Its deeper message reminds us to put the brakes on our negative thinking before our thoughts run out of control.

Our minds need a frequent tune–up to remain clear and able to see all the wonderful things in life.

We're OFF COURSE when:
- We build each negative thought into the worst–case scenario like a car without brakes, making no effort to slow down or redirect our thinking.
- The adrenaline of drama fuels us to the point of plaguing us with stress related illnesses.
- We tend to distract ourselves with addictions, and often don't pay attention to our state of health until it is too late.
- We become a victim of our own thinking when we see our fabricated thoughts as true, unwilling to recognize another perspective.
- We give more weight to our negative rather than our positive thoughts and feel overpowered by them.
- We seem intrigued by all of the negative events of the world, and focus on them as a way of numbing to our own.
- We believe worry is a form of caring, so the bigger our worry, the more we care.

We're ON COURSE when:
- We see worry as a useless waste of energy rather than genuine caring, and use gratitude, appreciation and meditation as antidotes to worry.
- We are committed to a present moment seeing.
- We recognize that our thoughts do not control us unless we give them the power to do so. The quality of our life is determined by the quality of our thoughts.

Travel Tips:

- Determine five areas where your life and your thoughts are in the 'run–away' mode. What can you do right now to make adjustments and fine tune your thinking?
- List the action steps you are willing to take, and by when, to make the adjustments to bring more calm and clarity back into your life.
- List five worries that distract you from living the fullest life possible.
- What are the concrete steps you can take to find a solution and to refocus you in the present moment?
- For every worry, list at least three things you are grateful for. Maintain a gratitude journal. End each day counting your blessings.
- Notice your own resistance. Shift to being willing, and forgive yourself.

CHAPTER TWENTY-TWO

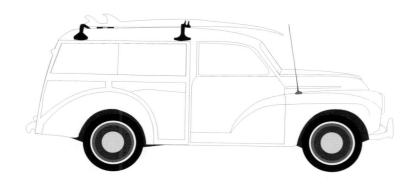

PARK–AND–RIDE
*Sometimes the strongest thing
we can do is ask for help.
Give and receive support
with gratitude. It's one of your most
important contributions.*

GENERALLY, OUR CULTURE HAS BEEN DETOURED in two different directions. Some of us travel a path of feeling unworthy of love and respect, and others move along the path of entitlement, feeling we are the only ones worthy of love and respect. We have either become over–givers, where we care for others more than we do ourselves, or we have become so self–absorbed that we perceive our needs to be more important than the needs of anyone else. Both paths lead us off course. To be happy we must return to a road where there is a balance of compassion, generosity, self–love, and willing personal responsibility. This is living with integrity.

Giving is not done to get something in return. If we give with expectations to get back, it is not a true gift and holds only fleeting satisfaction. We will not always receive from the people we think we should, when we should, or in the form we expect; however, we must trust that we will receive. The true gift lies in discovering value in the act of giving itself, without expecting anything in return.

Although it is always wonderful to receive, lasting happiness deepens when our heart is touched by the act of genuine giving. Love is the magic of that fused moment where generosity and gratitude meet. At some point on our journey we will have the opportunity to be a 'giver' and a 'receiver.' We serve one another when we learn to accept both with grace and authenticity.

We will benefit by being reminded to PARK–AND–RIDE.

Rather than feel as though we need to carry everyone else through life, we can learn the value of humility. We can reach out from time to time and accept help. Opening our willingness to accept support and riding together through life offers the advantage of the insight of another. Experiencing their unconditional love helps us to learn more about ourselves, blessed and relieved that we need not be alone.

We're OFF COURSE when:
- We feel entitled to have life go our way. Life is seen as a series of inconveniences and disappointments where we expect the worst.
- We are so focused on our perception of what is right that we miss other possibilities right before our eyes.
- We see asking as a sign of weakness.
- We find it hard to ask for help because we often don't really know what we want. We find it awkward to receive without feeling guilty, suspicious and lacking in trust.
- We are ineffective leaders and find fault in just about everything while seeing our criticisms as necessary, helpful, and constructive.
- We are perfectionists. We are demeaning of others and ourselves when our unrealistic expectations are not being met.
- We work even when we are sick. We extend beyond our limits physically, mentally and emotionally. We often don't even realize that we're jeopardizing our well-being, productivity, creativity, health, and our relationships by trying to 'do' life solo, until it is too late.
- We live life in a defensive mode and our self-worth is threatened by the creative contributions of others.
- We find it hard to accept compliments with grace and seldom do we offer acknowledgment to others.

We're ON COURSE when:

- We learn to ask for help without expectation, and receive it graciously as a means of refueling ourselves when our battery is low.
- We feel worthy of help and empower others by letting them lead the way. We learn to surround ourselves with those who are dependable, willing, and trustworthy and know that giving is a two–way street. We avoid people and situations causing self–sabotage.
- We suspend judgment and are open to brainstorming ideas before eliminating possibilities. We appreciate the viewpoints of others.
- We recognize the importance of maintaining balance in our lives, and realize that asking is a form of taking responsibility for creating what we need and want.
- Our goal is excellence, not perfection, for others and ourselves.

Travel Tips:

- List five areas in which you need help or where you feel overwhelmed. Practice delegating. Ask for help at least once today, even if it is in small ways, and even if you feel uncomfortable asking. Asking creates the opportunity for another to give, and in giving our life has greater meaning. Asking for help becomes a gift of opportunity for another to shine.
- Do not take rejection personally. Practice receiving a gift, even when the answer is NO, trusting that you are still worthwhile.
- Recognize that the other person also finds it a challenge to give and receive. 'Give em a brake' and make their giving easier with gratitude.
- Give anonymously and often. Simple gifts are often the most meaningful.
- At the end of your day today, determine what you gave, and what you received and appreciate both.

CHAPTER TWENTY-THREE

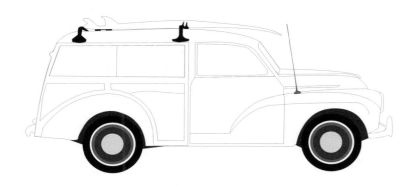

NO DUMPING
*Often, we are not upset
for the reason we think.
When we 'dump' on others,
it is a sign there is something
important to 'dump'
in our own way of thinking.*

WE ALL WOULD LIKE TO THINK OUR COMMUNICATION IS EFFECTIVE; however, just because we say something does not insure we were heard, and often means more than what was said. We give the words we speak a tremendous amount of power and proceed as is if communication is only semantics. We become numb to the genuine impact of what we say, and are often insensitive to what is implied or assumed. Sometimes one word, or even silence, is too much when thousands of words are not enough. With an awareness of the true intention of our communication, and by determining whether or not it matters to us how our message is received, we can make our words far more effective and heart–felt. We develop greater understanding that communication travels beyond mere words.

Only 8% of communication is accomplished by the words we speak. Certain words invite defensiveness regardless of our intention, while others welcome trust and understanding. Being sensitive also to what is not said offers a more accurate window into the heart and true meaning of another. This becomes easier when we expand our awareness of body language and inflections, validating our perception, and then seeing if the words and actions match.

Words are helpful, but without the congruent actions they are empty and meaningless. Given our human tendency to put our foot in our mouth, it's amazing we do as well as we do! It is learning to listen to the intentions and disguised truths beyond words that is important. When we take responsibility for what we say with and without words, we open the door to discovering the possibilities for meaning and joy, we deepen our happiness.

The road of life is more enjoyable when communication includes both speaking and listening. Happiness is ours when we take persistent steps toward both speaking and listening with greater care. Our compass pointed toward strong communication skills will lead us to experiencing the greater sense of calm and mutual respect that comes from feeling genuinely heard even when we are in disagreement.

Often we are reminded by a NO DUMPING sign to be conscious about where and how we vent our irritations. We need to remain aware of their impact on others and ourselves. Although we need a SOFT SHOULDER from time to time, someone who can compassionately listen to us 'dump' without judgment, we also benefit from releasing our negative thoughts and replace them by focusing on what's working. We need to listen for more than our turn to talk and forgive transgressions quickly to fully enjoy and appreciate the wonders of our journey.

We're OFF COURSE when:
- We are quick to criticize and limit ourselves by disputing details, missing the intended message and the advantage of seeing the big picture.
- Fear activates our defensiveness and we live life as one power struggle after another. We react as if people are out to get us or that no one understands.
- We blame others for our outbursts and shortcomings. We participate in gossip, and incite ill feelings.
- We feel entitled to having life our way, and are willing to insist it be so at the expense of another.

- We discount and invalidate, using the word 'but.' Example: "I hear what you are saying, *but* I have a better idea."
- We strive for a sense of personal power by treating others with little respect, making ourselves feel 'more than' by making sure they feel 'less than.'

We're ON COURSE when:
- We are accountable for the times we react rather than respond. We are quick to offer a heartfelt apology, and immediately adjust our behavior in the future.
- We become more sensitive to the impact of our words and actions on another, and become more conscious of our tendency to manipulate others to accept our point of view.
- We approach the things that bother us about another as an invitation to review and adjust where we are 'off course' in our own way of thinking. Irritations become valuable opportunities to expand our personal growth and enhance our positive perspective, helping us to bypass our limiting beliefs.
- We confront conflict with an intention to find resolution and peace, and sometimes agree to disagree without drama or the need for a power struggle. We choose being happy over being right.
- We apply reflective listening. We recognize that although it seems like it takes too much time, it ultimately will save time and insure more genuine communication, greater integrity, and stronger relationships.
- We find value in differences rather than seeing them as a threat that triggers defensiveness and suspicion.
- We validate the viewpoint of another, implementing the word 'and.' Example: "I hear what you are saying, *and* I have another idea."

Traveling Tips:
- Notice all the times you include the word 'but' when you are exchanging ideas and attempting to resolve a problem. Understand the word 'but' often invites defensiveness.
- Consciously practice substituting the word 'and' in the place of 'but.' Experience how 'and' is a word that invites sharing, trust, and willingness and expands your ability to see the viewpoint of another.
- Practice listening beyond words and validating that you heard the essence of their communication before responding.
- Yielding to genuine and mutual communication makes the journey of life far more enjoyable and you seldom travel alone.

CHAPTER TWENTY–FOUR

DETOUR

*Being 'off course' is an integral part
of being 'on course,'
and failure is an essential part
of success.*

WE GET VERY UPSET WHEN WE VEER 'OFF COURSE.' Frustrated by the inconvenience of the deviation from our plans, we resist the acknowledgement of our detour and continue ahead determined to get to the destination we want. If you don't know where you are going, any road will get you there. We proceed unwilling to ask for directions, uncertain where we are headed or why, and too busy being upset to notice the road signs available to return us to the main road more easily.

Our purpose in life is honed by our core values and gives us a sense of meaning around which we establish a malleable path for our life. It acts like a compass that alerts us when we deviate too far from our optimum route. It offers us a reference point from which we can choose again a new direction or to find our way back to our course all the stronger for our detour.

Daring to declare a purpose offers us a deeper insight of who we are that reaches beyond the limitations of being human. It gives us a context from which to appreciate where we came from, an understanding of how we got here, a consciousness about where we are going, and a sense of how we might best determine a destination congruent to the true value of our journey. It offers a trellis for our happiness. It supports our awareness that the quality of each step is as important as the destination. Happiness is a style of traveling, not a place at which we arrive. It is a moment–by–moment choice enjoyed as a process, not something we only get at the end of the ride. Why wait?

The process of life is often a messy and imperfect one We deviate or get distracted now and then from our intended direction by choice or by circumstance. Not to worry, although we often do. Seldom do we make it through life without a bit of backtracking or an unplanned side trip. We need not resist mistakes and side roads. They offer valuable feedback which helps us determine our optimum path. It's important to accept that failure is a necessary ingredient as we create success. Ask Thomas Edison, Jonas Salk, the Wright brothers, Helen Keller, or a baby learning to walk. If we see our detours as opportunities to improve and accept ourselves, rather than as failures that limit us, we adjust our course with grace and begin again to enjoy the journey with joy regardless of the circumstances.

Our purpose in life need not be grandiose to be meaningful. A purpose as simple as being loving every day, making a difference in the life of another, raising a grateful child, or daily acts with integrity, is a tremendous contribution. Small steps lead to huge and positive change. Regardless of the size or form it takes, the value of our path lies in the love with which we take each step and implement each dream. We all are not meant to discover the cure for cancer. Happiness is ours consistently when we accept and celebrate that we are always in the right place at the right time. Your purpose becomes your reference guide for making decisions along the way.

Each time we see a DETOUR sign, let us be reminded that being off course is a valuable and necessary part of being on course. Wandering away from our intended route is a chance to fine-tune our ability to recognize our path back again. Finding our way back after being lost strengthens our ability to know more clearly what our true course is. Conscious DETOURS can be wise adventures. Unconscious DETOURS can be opportunities to choose again. What really matters is that we remain willing and open to participate fully in whatever the adventure of life has to offer with arms wide open and our faith in gear.

We're OFF COURSE when:
- We are distracted from our own sense of direction by trying to travel the path outlined for us by others, or we live another's path for them. We struggle to live up to someone else's definition of success, losing sight of our own values and priorities, or judge others by our criteria for success.
- Seeing mistakes as failure, we cover up our shortcomings rather than use them as a reference point for clarification and growth.
- We fail to see life as a process where progress is not always a continuous road forward, but sometimes involves steps backward or a change in the direction we thought we were headed in favor of an alternate route.
- We are inflexible and fearful of change. We react, resist and cling to what is familiar even when it no longer works.
- We are so focused on the destination that the twists and turns of the journey frighten us. We miss obvious opportunities for love and success.

We're ON COURSE when:
- We see value in setting goals and aiming for a specific outcome, and we balance that desire with a willingness to notice signs, signals, and inner wisdom along the way which sometimes redirects our journey in a new direction.
- We see life as an adventure of learning and change as a part of the process. We anticipate situations that will demand us to stretch, grow, and be challenged.
- We do not get stuck in self–criticism of our mistakes and detours, but free ourselves by forgiving our setbacks quickly. We create value in a mistake by applying what we have learned to the next situation. We return quickly to our path with greater commitment clarity.

- We know that life is too serious to take it all seriously. We add lightheartedness and humor to the journey.

Travel Tips:
- What are the bottom line most important things to you? Define your sense of purpose. What would give your life direction and meaning?
- List five areas you feel you are 'off course.'
- What are the clues that signal you are 'off course.'
- Prioritize and recommit to your values. List five specific steps that will allow your actions to be purposeful and meaningful. Make them SMART and be willing and flexible along the way.

S	=	Specific	What do you want?
M	=	Measurable	What determines if you've succeeded?
A	=	Attainable	Is it chucked down into doable steps?
R	=	Relevant	Does it relate to your purpose?
T	=	Time	When will you reach each step?

- Remember not to focus on your setbacks. Forgive yourself quickly, be SMART, gather necessary clues for future advances, and welcome the opportunity to learn by adjusting your course. Applaud your new awareness and celebrate even small steps in your renewed direction, enjoying simple pleasures along the way.
- List five simple pleasures.
- List five incremental successes. How are you going to celebrate your next step forward?

CHAPTER TWENTY–FIVE

ENTER
*Strength and wisdom come
when we make our decisions
from the inside out.
Drive–in.*

MANY OF OUR DECISIONS ARE PRESSURED BY TIME and driven by guilt, fear, or anger. We avoid them thinking we always have to be right. We depend on others to make them for us, often losing sight of what we want. We falsely believe that the answers are outside of us somewhere, and life remains a quest. We forget that love is the answer to every question, and that when we ENTER our own heart we access our own inner strength and intuition.

I have made some pretty bad decisions in my life. Haven't we all! The good news is that there is no such thing as a bad decision if we listen within, lead with our good intentions, are willing to risk in order to grow, and consciously apply what we learn from our mistakes. Life becomes an adventure of sculpting our purpose and making a difference. It is an easier journey when we accept it as a messy process that is hard and unpredictable sometimes. When we learn how to surrender to the mystery of life including its uncertainties we become stronger, see more possibilities, expand our capabilities, gain clarity and create miracles. The quality of each present moment becomes preferable to being numb and living life on cruise control.

The ENTER sign becomes a reminder to look within for answers. Our power resides within. Be willing to drive–in and rediscover the value of being still and to hear your own wisdom. Trust it.

We're OFF COURSE when:

- We hesitate to take risks and play life safe instead. We lack confidence in our decisions, and make them by succumbing to the demands of others. Striving for perfection and acceptance, we over–analyze every decision, and fail to trust our inner sense of knowing what is best for us.
- We hesitate saying 'no' for fear of not being liked. Instead of being direct, we feel resentful and join the 'martyr's union.'
- We say 'yes,' but are filled with resentment.
- Guilt and blame are our traveling companions.
- We blame others for our undesirable outcomes.

We're ON COURSE when:

- We realize that not making a decision is making a decision.
- We trust that every decision is the right one regardless of how it appears. Even mistakes offer information that helps us grow, therefore, we realize we are always in the right place at the right time. There is no reason to be impatient with circumstances beyond our control.
- We forgive ourselves for mistakes and consciously apply what we learn to the next opportunity.
- We know that our strongest answers lie within. We acknowledge the value of our intuition and balance it with logic. We have faith in our intuition, dare to take reasonable risks, and make decisions from the 'inside out.'
- We dare to say 'no,' trusting that an honest 'no' is better than a half–hearted 'yes' even when we disappoint someone.
- We willingly say 'yes,' even when it's inconvenient, as an opportunity to stretch beyond our comfort zone. We know there is always a gift in the giving that outweighs our inconvenience.

Travel Tips:

- Make conscious choices and be willing to take reasonable risks.
- Listen for and reconnect with the inner voice that has been dominated by your logic. Honor it well for it is an essential traveling companion on the road of happiness.
- Let logic and intuition become playmates on the teeter–totter of life.
- Lighten up when making even serious decisions, knowing that mistakes will offer you an opportunity to learn and creativity is shut down when fear is present.

Heads or tails

Think of something you need to decide, but are uncertain about. Now, flip a coin and call it in the air. Notice your reaction when it lands. Were you glad it was 'heads?' Or, are you willing to settle for 'heads,' even though you have a reaction that 'tails' might have been the better choice? Use a coin toss not as a tool to make a decision for you, but as a way of giving yourself a deeper inner sense of what you really want. Pay more attention to the inner signal, than the outcome of any coin toss. It's really about expanding your ability to listen to the real voice within.

Questions for decision making

Deciding to decide is often the hardest part of making any decision. The following questions will help you clarify your thoughts and plan your actions leading you to make decisions with greater confidence.

- Why must I decide, and what is my real goal?
- What is my bottom line? Have I listened to my 'gut?
- What is my greatest fear?
- What will make me feel the most empowered?

111

- By when must I decide?
- What new information do I need before I decide?
- Can I chunk the decision down into smaller steps?
- Can I change my mind, or is this decision final?
- What risks are involved, and are they worth it?
- Am I willing to have excellence rather than perfection?
- Am I willing to know that 'right' or 'wrong,' there is a perfect gift? What is the gift? Focus on it.

CHAPTER TWENTY–SIX

WEIGHT LIMIT

*We can wait longer,
and handle the weight
of not getting what we want
more than we think we can.
Practice patience; learn to let go
with grace, and trust that life
is as it is meant to be.*

WE THINK THAT WE CAN BE HAPPY ONLY WHEN LIFE IS EASY and we have things go our way. The daily responsibilities seem too much of a burden sometimes. Agitated by the pressures of life, we often go numb with self–doubt and hesitate slowing down enough to be right here right now, insisting on just being 'right' instead. With our demand that life be predictable we miss an important opportunity to dance with adversity and to make friends with change. We do avoidance, a–void–dance. We hide in a void and run from adversity rather than face it. Happiness is ours if we are lucky enough to learn we can dance even in a void!

It's the hardest times, the unexpected deviations that often become our greatest teachers. They introduce us to a part of ourselves and a sense of our strength that we otherwise would not know. When we realize that life includes good and bad times, joy and grief, delay and flow, it allows us to apply our courage, and experience our ability to be happy regardless of the circumstances. Happiness is durable and embraces grief, disappointment, excitement, relief, pain and joy.

We are always stronger than we think. Imagine what it would be like if we actually believed we were capable, and always in the right place at the right time. We would see life as friendly, regardless of how we distorted it by our misper-ceptions. We would handle change and challenge with greater grace and resilience, and have an abundance of wonderful opportunities limited only by our degree of willingness to grow.

Appreciate each WEIGHT LIMIT road sign as a reminder that your magnificence is limitless. Committed to joy you will be able to carry the WEIGHT of challenging situations with more grace, and WAIT with greater patience knowing that all things are as they are meant to be regardless of how they appear. It also is a reminder to lighten your load, adjust your attitude and lighten up by expanding your sense of humor.

We're OFF COURSE when:
- We expect immediate gratification and are totally thrown 'off course' when life does not go as planned. We find it hard to wait, crumble in a crisis, and over–react under pressure.
- We often are rude, arrogant, and when forced to wait we often use humiliation as a form of manipulation to regain a sense of control. We generally place our needs above the needs of others. We never feel like people do enough for us.
- We over–react, turning small things into a drama. We avoid challenges and take the easy way out and seldom rise to the occasion.
- We forfeit our sense of humor for sarcasm. Without light–heartedness life weighs us down and makes any wait longer and more intolerable.

We're ON COURSE when:
- Laughter becomes a valuable tool which allows us to sur-render more easily to the unexplainable parts of life. A sense of humor helps us tolerate things that don't go as we expect.
- We embrace change as just a part of the human experience that need not be feared. We handle adversity with grace, welcoming the lessons it brings.

- We accept loss as a part of the cycle of life that strengthens us and know there is a gift in even the most challenging time. We learn to let go, trusting grief and detachment as a process that will teach us more about how capable we are.
- We expect and accept forward and backward steps as progress toward our goals. We expand our WAIT LIMIT, using setbacks as an opportunity to practice patience. We expand our WEIGHT LIMIT, realizing that even when we feel we have reached our capacity, we are stronger and more capable than we think we are. There always is a valuable lesson to be gained from our endurance and persistence.

I fully understand that God will not give me more than I can handle. I just wish He didn't trust me so much.

—Mother Teresa

Travel Tips:
- What if you were in the right place at the right time regardless of how it appeared? Try on that belief for a few days and become the detective to discover the opportunities right before your very eyes.
- Commit to do something inconvenient daily, and choose to do it willingly and joyfully, until you can appreciate the extraordinary in the ordinary and see the value in being right here right now.
- Admit your limitations and take good care of yourself to acquire the energy necessary to choose to stretch beyond what you resist.

Letting Go

To let go does not mean to stop caring;
it means I can't do it for someone else.
To let go is not to cut myself off;
it's the realization that I can't control another.
To let go is not to enable,
 but to allow leaning from natural consequences.
To let go is to admit powerlessness,
which means the outcome is not in my hands.
To let go is not to try to change or blame another.
I can only change myself.
To let go is not to care for,
but to care about.
To let go is not to fix,
but to be supportive.
To let go is not to judge,
but to allow another to be a human being.
To let go is not to be in the middle
arranging all the outcomes,
but to allow others to affect their own outcomes.
To let go is not to be protective,
It is to permit another to face reality.
To let go is not to deny, but to accept.
To let go is not to nag, scold, or argue,
but to search out my own shortcomings and correct them.
To let go is not to adjust everything to my desires,
but to take each day as it comes and cherish the moment.
To let go is not to criticize and regulate anyone,
but to try to become what I dream I can be.
To let go is not to address the past,
but to grow and live for the future.
To let go is to fear less and love more.

—Author Unknown

116

CHAPTER TWENTY–SEVEN

DIP

Depression is a dip in our perspective.
Our low spot does not allow us to ask
for help or see the progress we've made.
Breakdowns happen.
Breakthroughs are possible.

EVERYONE GOES THROUGH A TIME when we lose our perspective and see the road of life as more treacherous than it is. We become a DIP, a Dysfunctionally Independent Person. We trap ourselves in our unwillingness to see anything but the low side of life. When depressed we feel like we hit a patch of ice. We slip and slide out of control with no traction. We are thrown into a state of survival, disillusionment and despair, and lose our confidence, creativity and compassion in our tailspin.

Although our circumstances can be very tough and seem overwhelming at times, we usually succeed in making them worse than they need to be when we hit a stretch of catastrophe thinking. Even in the worst of times all we really need to handle is this moment, and then the next second, and then another, until with as much love as we can muster. As we reconnect with our willingness we will reconnect with our ability to move through our fear.

DIP signs appear often as a way of remembering to see above the low spot and shift our perception to what's working. Gratitude and authentic action are the means to re–establish our direction. Reaching out when we least feel like it is an important antidote to depression, and counteracts our tendency to live as a DIP, a **D**ysfunctionally **I**ndependent **P**erson.

We're OFF COURSE when:

- We live in a depression that can be described as anger without enthusiasm. We are disappointed by life and yet have grown numb rather than face our upset.
- We use alcohol, food, sex, T.V. and other avenues to cover up our despair, fearful that nothing can be done about it and afraid that no one will care enough to help.
- We ignore initial signals that we are 'off course.' We attempt to force the outcome to be as we want it rather than welcoming it as an opportunity to learn.
- Our self–esteem deteriorates without regular care and maintenance, and we often accommodate the needs of others to the exclusion of our own. We often see ourselves as inadequate and less important.
- We wallow in our discontent and fail to take the actions to be with the people who support us in the renewal of our Spirit.
- We isolate ourselves as a DIP.

We're ON COURSE when:

- Depression signals we are 'off course.' Recognizing that FEAR has gotten the better of us, we take exceptional care of ourselves and ask for help if necessary. We readjust our life to our values despite our tendency to hide. We don't resist the dips, but flow with them and accept them as a reminder to appreciate the even pavement along the way.
- We acknowledge our anger and disappointment, but don't dramatize it. We search for our misperceptions and negative thinking, and are eager to adjust old patterns, look for the gift created by the challenge, and to regain a more positive perspective.
- We chunk down things that feel overwhelming until the steps are manageable, and take small and persistent steps forward while accepting there will be steps backward.

- We refuel with positive sources of inspiration, time alone, a calm environment, time in nature, and nurturing experiences.
- We reach out and ask for help, building a healthy support system.

Travel Tips:
- It serves us to always be willing to review our choices. It helps us to adjust our perspective by asking ourselves: What's the worst that could happen? Am I using catastrophe thinking?
- Are the circumstances **F**alse **E**xpectations **A**ppearing **R**eal?
- Am I taking myself or someone else too seriously?
- What small steps can I take to lighten up and focus on what is working?
- Where am I over–reacting rather than responding?
- How can I lovingly accept my shortcomings as an essential part of who I am rather than resist them and see myself as inadequate?
- Where can I adjust my negative thinking and refocus on the present moment?
- What am I grateful for?
- Who do I need to forgive?
- What can I learn from this experience?
- Where am I off course?
- Where have I abandoned my values?
- How can I apply what I am now aware of to make my words and actions match my values?
- When we are depressed, we are often highly unmotivated. Still, action toward renewing our spirit is essential to move from a breakdown to breakthrough to get back on the freeway.

We must ACT:
- A = Acknowledge our despair, frustration and anger.
- C = Consciously choose a different attitude so our words and actions match our values.
- T = Transform our fears and disappointments with a positive perspective and present moment seeing.

CHAPTER TWENTY–EIGHT

SPEED BUMP AHEAD

The speed bumps in our life
are often wake–up calls
to value what is right before our eyes.
If ignored or resisted, they get bigger,
often leading to a slide area
with falling rocks!

PROCRASTINATORS ARE OFTEN PERFECTIONISTS IN DISGUISE. We delay beginning until we think we can do it perfectly. We ignore problems and bumps in life when they are small, hoping they will disappear, but instead they escalate and accumulate to a point of chaos.

It's time to avoid chaos by slowing down to notice the signals offered by life warning us to tune our engine, recharge our battery and put spark back in our plugs before we reach a point of breakdown. By slowing down and tuning in, we actually renew our spirit in a way that allows us to go faster, make better decisions and get better mileage out of our energy. We must remember that it is what's under the hood and in your heart that offers us dependable happiness.

Every SPEED BUMP warning can act as a reminder to slow down enough to recognize how life is attempting to support us in our happiness. It is not how fast we finish life that matters, but the quality of the journey that is of the greatest importance.

We're OFF COURSE when:
- We live life on the surface and focus on quantity, not quality. We live life in the fast lane with the misperception that more and faster is better.
- We expect life to be smooth, feel like a victim when it's not, and attempt to control challenges and change to force our preferred outcome.

- We ignore small warnings, and choose to live in denial. Rather than face a problem we distract ourselves until it has escalated to a major roadblock.
- We depend on adrenaline rushes, caffeine, drugs or another addiction to maintain our accelerated pace.
- We are cynical, and have little patience and compassion.

We're ON COURSE when:
- We pay attention to our body's signals to slow down, and see them as opportunities stay aware and to appreciate what is right before us rather than rushing so fast through life that we miss the extraordinary in the ordinary.
- We keep life simple and our communication clear. We address misunderstandings immediately, rather than letting them fester and grow out of proportion.
- We take the time to listen intently, honor the feelings of others, and savor simple pleasures knowing that the most important things in life aren't things.
- We handle the falling rocks of problems and challenging issues before they become an avalanche of boulders.
- We recognize that in slowing down enough to make conscious adjustments we become more effective, productive, efficient, and energized.

Travel Tips: ask yourself...
- What's the problem I'm always ignoring, or the project I'm always putting off?
- What small, certain and incremental steps will I take to address this problem? By when?
- Where can I slow down more in my life and appreciate music, nature, and the beauty that is present in things as simple as the smile of a baby?
- What are things you want to do with your family? With friends? With your partner? By yourself? What are you waiting for?

CHAPTER TWENTY–NINE

CHILDREN–AT–PLAY

Find delight even in scary moments.
Fasten your seat belt
and put your hands up in the air
on the roller coaster of life.

DO YOU REMEMBER THE LAST TIME YOU WERE LAUGHING so hard that you just couldn't stop? When we have a heartfelt belly laugh all sorts of wonderful things happen. Laughter decreases pain, creates a bonding experience, encourages creativity, exercises our lungs, releases endorphins, lifts our spirits and makes even a good time better. It not only is a gift to our self, but a gift to others, too. Life is too serious to take it all seriously.

Life is seldom easy, but always simple when we know that love is the solution to every problem. Still, we avoid the hard parts of life whenever we can. The truth is we cannot prevent pain, nor would we want to for it is often a profound way of learning lasting wisdom. We all experience misfortune and painful times, some more than others. Playfulness and a sense of humor allows us to laugh at challenges as soon as possible after they happen, heal from pain that seemed unbearable, and transform adversity into valued gifts that make us better people.

Playing in life and with life can be our reminder when we see a CHILDREN AT PLAY road sign. Take every opportunity to reconnect with your innocence, lightheartedness, and delight. Play is an important avenue to happiness. To experience durable happiness it serves us to integrate play into our work, our relationships, our intimate moments, and our alone time. If all else fails, find a mentor under the age of four!

We're OFF COURSE when:

- We take life too seriously and don't like feeling out of control.
- We like to know the outcome of any situation before we begin.
- We seldom take risks, disdain mistakes, and are quick to blame others.
- We see work as serious business, and feel that spontaneity distracts from productivity and should be discouraged.
- We are inflexible, seldom laugh, and find the normal antics of children a bother rather than entertaining and refreshing.
- We are suspicious of people who seem to be enjoying life, and are certain that they can't possibly be working hard enough.

We're ON COURSE when:

- We look for ways of infusing playful moments into even the most pressing deadlines knowing that work without play and lightheartedness will lead to burn–out.
- We smile often and without cause, and in so doing find even more to smile about.
- We look for opportunities to be spontaneous and to renew a childlike spirit.
- We regard people with innocence, trusting their positive intention, and expect the best from them.
- We laugh often, enjoy people who do, and infuse our life with a sense of humor.
- We see life as a 'win–win' game.

Travel Tips:

- Dare to enjoy things like skipping, swinging, or singing to yourself in the car.
- Dare to have a best friend.

- Place a 'play' date on your calendar where you do something frivolous and wonderful for yourself.
- Have a Saturday comedy day, watching all funny movies.
- Try any one of the "31 Flavors" you have not tried.
- Read the comics before the stock market report.
- Ride a roller coaster, with your hands up!
- Eat dessert first tonight!

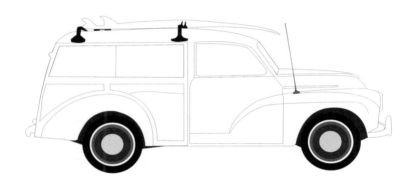

Conclusion: The End is the Beginning

This may be the end of this book, but certainly not the end of the road. Exactly when is our journey complete? One of my favorite books is *Illusions: The Adventures of a Reluctant Messiah*, Dell Publishing, a Division of Random House. In it Richard Bach, through his character, Donald Shamoda, offers us a practical measurement.

"Here is the test to find whether your mission on earth is finished: If you're alive, it isn't."

The human part of life is an ever–changing journey full of incredible lessons and unexpected gifts, not a certain and predictable destination. It is not a pursuit of something out there, but a process of appreciating the extraordinary that is right before us and deep within us. It is not an effort of self–improvement, but rather the discovery that peace and happiness is defined by self–acceptance and a remembering of who we really already innately are.

Reading this book does not mean that we have now 'arrived' or that our journey will ever be over. It does not mean that our adventure will be without potholes and detours. It is offered as a traveling companion to remind us that we already are magnificent, that happiness is a choice, and that signs of happiness surround us, if you are willing to enjoy and implement them. Greater simplicity and success are ours when we choose over and over again to have our words and actions match and to remember that love is the answer to every question. These tools guarantee that no matter what road you travel and no matter how long your path, your adventure can be a joy ride.

You get to chart your course by following your heart. Remember to *DRIVE YOURSELF HAPPY* by being here NOW, traveling lighthearted, and knowing that it is what's under the hood that counts.

A QUICK FIX for DEPRESSION
and a JUMP START for HAPPINESS

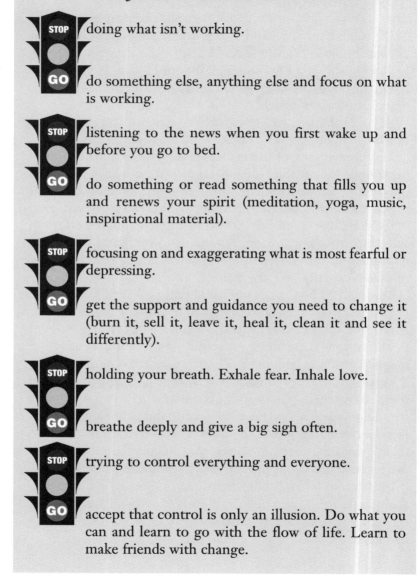

STOP doing what isn't working.

GO do something else, anything else and focus on what is working.

STOP listening to the news when you first wake up and before you go to bed.

GO do something or read something that fills you up and renews your spirit (meditation, yoga, music, inspirational material).

STOP focusing on and exaggerating what is most fearful or depressing.

GO get the support and guidance you need to change it (burn it, sell it, leave it, heal it, clean it and see it differently).

STOP holding your breath. Exhale fear. Inhale love.

GO breathe deeply and give a big sigh often.

STOP trying to control everything and everyone.

GO accept that control is only an illusion. Do what you can and learn to go with the flow of life. Learn to make friends with change.

STOP being so hard on yourself for imperfections.

GO strive for excellence, not perfection.

STOP clinging to unrealistic expectations.

GO set manageable goals and celebrate incremental steps.

STOP sitting on the 'pity potty' feeling sorry for yourself.

GO find a way to assist others and be of service where you can contribute your talents, time and resources.

STOP reliving the past you can't change and worrying about the future that may not happen.

GO enjoy this precious present moment.

STOP waiting until you feel like it or until it's too late.

GO enjoy life now. It is the only moment you really have.

STOP being lethargic and reclusive.

GO walk, run, swing, square dance, swim for at least 20 minutes a day.

TICKET

to being happy regardless of your circumstances

Highway Patrol
(Looking for a higher way of being)

No. 2BEHERENOW

NOTICE TO APPEAR
(Showing up authentically, willing to grow and handle change with grace)

Name: _____ Who drives your car: CIRCUMSTANCES / ME

Mailing Address: _____

City: _____ State: _____ ZIP: _____

Recent number of happiness violations: _____ Birthday: _____

Attitude: (Circle) POSITIVE / NEGATIVE

Degree of willingness: (Circle) 1 2 3 4 5 6 7 8 9 10

Estimated amount of time currently living in the present moment:
(Circle) none 1 2 3 4 5 6 7 8 9 all

Current distractions from and major
VIOLATIONS of being happy:

- ❑ Reliving the past with resentment
- ❑ Living life in the fast lane
- ❑ Inability to forgive self / others
- ❑ Procrastinator
- ❑ Road rage reactions and outbursts
- ❑ Traveling in the state of confusion
- ❑ Backseat driving
- ❑ Out of balance
- ❑ Wrong way driving
- ❑ Words and actions don't match
- ❑ Unrealistic expectations of self / others

- ❑ Judgmental of self / others
- ❑ Not signaling before lane change
- ❑ Perfectionist
- ❑ Loss of compassion for self / others
- ❑ Running out of gas
- ❑ Stuck in a rut
- ❑ Riding the worry wheel
- ❑ Driving against the flow of traffic
- ❑ Unclear priorities
- ❑ Tailgating
- ❑ Just plain being a jerk

Items checked are issued pursuant to *DRIVE YOURSELF HAPPY* and refer to the motor-vational maintenance manual's vehicle code recommendations for personal and professional success in happily maneuvering through life. See book for clearance procedures.

Inspected by:

Date of inspection:

Driver's definition of happiness and success: _____

Strategy for how to ADOPT-A-HIGHWAY: _____

Priorities for driving happy:

1. _____

2. _____

3. _____

I certify under the penalty of mediocrity that the foregoing is true and correct, and assessed with love and compassion on the date shown above at (place):

Issuing Officer/Driving Instructor:

Signature:

Rhonda Hull, Ph.D.
P.O. Box 1639
Port Hadlock, WA 98368
Work: 360.385.5850
Fax: 360.385.5865

DRIVE YOURSELF HAPPY

Rhonda Hull

m

Declaration of action steps that will be implemented to create balance, offer forgiveness and respond rather than react to get back on course and back in the driver's seat of life with joy:

1. _____

2. _____

3. _____

SURRENDERING GUILT, BLAME, RESISTANCE, AND CATASTROPHIC THINKING, I PROMISE TO SHOW UP IN LIFE IN A WHOLE NEW WAY, EVEN IF TAKING SMALL STEPS. I PROMISE TO FOCUS ON EVERYTHING THAT IS WORKING IN MY LIFE WITH AN ATTITUDE OF GRATITUDE.

X SIGNATURE

QUICK ORDER FORM

Toll Free: **800.773.7782** Fax: **707.964.7531**
Have your credit card ready.
E-mail orders: info@cypresshouse.com
Postal orders: Cypress House
              155 Cypress Street
              Fort Bragg, CA 95437 USA

Please send me _____ book(s) at $14.95 each US
                                      $20.95 each Canada

Please send more FREE information on: Speaking/Seminars
Consulting, Retreats and Promotional Products.

Please add me to your mailing list: (circle one) Yes   No

Name:_____

Billing Address: _____

City: _____ State: ____ Zip: _____

Telephone: _____

E–mail:_____

Sales tax: California residents add 7.25%
Shipping: US: First Book: Book Rate $3.00, UPS or Priority
Mail $5.00. Each Additional Book $1.00.
International Shipping $10.00 per book.

Payment: Check   VISA   MasterCard
(circle one)
Card number: _____

Name on card:_____

Expiration date:_____

Signature: _____

_____